Doubt and the Demands of Democratic Citizenship

The triumph of democracy has been heralded as one of the greatest achievements of the twentieth century, yet it seems to be in a relatively fragile condition in the United States, if one is to judge by the proliferation of editorials, essays, and books that focus on public cynicism about politics and distrust of government. *Doubt and the Demands of Democratic Citizenship* explores the reasons for public discontent and proposes an account of democratic citizenship appropriate for a robust democracy. David Hiley argues that citizenship is more than simply participating in the electoral process. It requires a capacity to participate in the deliberative process with other citizens who might disagree fundamentally, a capacity that combines deep convictions with a willingness to subject those convictions to doubt through democratic decision making. Hiley develops his argument by examining the connection between doubt and democracy generally, as well as through case studies of Socrates, Montaigne, and Rousseau, interpreting them in light of contemporary issues.

David R. Hiley is professor of philosophy at the University of New Hampshire. He has held administrative academic positions at several North American universities and is the author of *Philosophy in Question: Essays on Pyrrhonian Themes* and is coeditor of *The Interpretative Turn: Philosophy, Science, and Culture* and *Richard Rorty*.

Doubt and the Demands of Democratic Citizenship

DAVID R. HILEY
University of New Hampshire

CAMBRIDGE
UNIVERSITY PRESS

CAMBRIDGE UNIVERSITY PRESS
Cambridge, New York, Melbourne, Madrid, Cape Town, Singapore, São Paulo

Cambridge University Press
32 Avenue of the Americas, New York, NY 10013-2473, USA

www.cambridge.org
Information on this title: www.cambridge.org/9780521865692

First published 2006

Printed in the United States of America

A catalog record for this publication is available from the British Library.

Library of Congress Cataloging in Publication Data
Hiley, David R.
Doubt and the demands of democratic citizenship / David R. Hiley.
p.   cm.
Includes bibliographical references (p.   ) and index.
ISBN 0-521-86569-7 (hardcover) – ISBN 0-521-68451-x (pbk.)
1. Skepticism.   2. Citizenship – United States.   3. Democracy –
United States.   I. Title.
B837.H545   2006
323.601–dc22   2005033364

ISBN-13   978-0-521-86569-2 hardback
ISBN-10   0-521-86569-7 hardback

ISBN-13   978-0-521-68451-4 paperback
ISBN-10   0-521-68451-x paperback

For Angela with love

Contents

vii

Preface

Several years ago I met an artist from a small community outside of Richmond, Virginia. He was producing what he called his Doubt Project. As part of the project he had invited everyone in his community for afternoon tea. At the tea he served sugar cookies molded in a puffy script spelling out "doubt." I know only a little about his artistic intention. It is just as well that I don't know more because it was enough that I was captivated by the idea that doubt was a value of a community and that it should be celebrated. It resonated with my philosophical outlook and I wanted to leave it at that.

Doubt has occupied my thinking for the last three decades. In 1988, I wrote a book that argued that skepticism was best understood as a way of life rather than a set of technical arguments about the possibility of knowledge; and its challenge is more political than epistemological.[1] During the course of that book I formulated what I called the *deep challenge of skepticism*: Can I live with fundamental doubts about the basis of my beliefs and values and, at the same time, live with the conviction and resoluteness that political responsibility requires? Can a skeptical way of life be a politically responsible life? A skeptical outlook seems to undermine the very foundations on which political criticism depends, or so it is often claimed. If this is the case, must the skeptic – lacking the certainty of an outside standpoint to justify a political stance – simply

---

[1] David R. Hiley, *Philosophy in Question: Essays on a Pyrrhonian Theme* (Chicago: University of Chicago Press, 1988).

have to acquiesce in the status quo? This book returns to these questions, placing them this time within the context of thinking about the nature of democracy and democratic citizenship. However, it has come about as a result of a long detour.

For the past fifteen years or so I have served in administrative roles at several universities while practicing philosophy on the side. But as I hope to make clear by the final chapter of this book, this detour has been important to my philosophical reflections about the challenges of skepticism. Universities have provided me with a laboratory in which to observe and think, and also to apply some of what I have learned about democratic theory to the culture of universities. More importantly, I have come to appreciate the distinctive role of universities in a democracy. My administrative roles forced me to think about philosophy in practice, philosophy and education, and education's democratic possibilities.

In returning to questions about the political implications of doubt, my thinking has also been shaped by the condition of political and civic culture in America today. What was earlier a primarily scholarly project has increasingly become my attempt to make sense of the strains and fissures in our democracy at the beginning of the new century. It goes without saying that the most recent presidential election in the United States dramatized the degree to which we are polarized around conflicting views about the role of the United States in the world, about the place of government in our lives, and about the values that should be central to our culture. It goes without saying because it has been said so much by the pundit class that we have come to accept polarization as merely the cultural landscape. But organizing our geography in terms of red and blue states is much too simpleminded because it overstates marginal differences in some areas and understates others. It goes without saying that distrust and disaffection characterize the American citizenry, even while acknowledging that there was the largest voter turnout in the recent presidential election than in any election in recent memory. Voting, however, is a necessary, but not a sufficient, condition for a healthy democracy. This is one of the lessons we should be learning from the democratization experiment in Iraq. As heartening as it was to see Iraqis risking all to go to the polls for the first time in decades, democracy is as much about the values of a culture and the character of its citizens than it is about the ballot.

Given the cynicism and distrust of politics in the United States, there is as much reason to worry about the quality of democratic culture here as there is to worry about the possibility of democratic culture in the Middle East.

I believe that the philosophical questions that motivated my earlier thinking about the political implications of skepticism are relevant for thinking about the nature of democracy, and also about how we might think differently about reinvigorating our democratic culture, thinking that does not paint our political lives as red or blue.

During my administrative sojourn, I was allowed time off from my responsibilities at important periods in my thinking about this project. I am grateful to Grace Harris, Provost Emeritus at Virginia Commonwealth University, for supporting an administrative sabbatical at the early stages of this book. I am also grateful to Joan Leitzel, President Emeritus of the University of New Hampshire, for an administrative sabbatical that made possible the final stage of this project. And I am especially grateful to her for how she modeled the best values of democratic decision making and how she articulated the responsibility universities have to the larger communities of which they are a part.

Some of my ideas have been tested in print along the way. Some ideas in Chapter 4 appeared in "The Politics of Skepticism: Reading Montaigne," *History of Philosophy Quarterly*, 9 (1992). Some ideas in Chapter 5 appeared in "The Individual and the General Will: Rousseau Reconsidered," *History of Philosophy Quarterly*, 7 (1990). And some ideas in Chapter 6 appeared in "The Democratic Purposes of General Education," *Liberal Education*, 82 (1996).

Finally, I am grateful to students and colleagues in the Philosophy Department at the University of New Hampshire who not only welcomed me back from my administrative detour but stimulated me to complete this book. I was able to test out parts of this project in an undergraduate seminar on democracy and its challenges and in two departmental colloquia in which students and colleagues were both sufficiently tolerant and aggressively challenging to force me to be clearer and more consistent. But more than that, their interest encouraged me to think that the project was worthwhile.

Introduction

It has become obligatory when writing about democracy these days to reflect on the paradoxical condition it has found itself in at the turn of this century. Democratization has been heralded as the triumph of the last century internationally. Yet it seems to be in a relatively fragile condition in the United States if one is to judge by the proliferation of editorials, essays, and books analyzing "democracy's discontents."

When asked what he thought was the most important thing that happened in the twentieth century, Nobel Prize economist Amartya Sen responded that it was "the emergence of democracy as the preeminently acceptable form of governance."[1] Francis Fukuyama, to offer another example, confidently asserted in *The End of History and the Last Man* that the collapse of authoritarianism and socialism during the last half of the twentieth century has left "only one competitor standing in the ring as an ideology of potentially universal validity: liberal democracy, the doctrine of individual freedom and popular sovereignty."[2] Certainly the number of democratic countries has increased if we are to judge by the expansion of popular elections. The executive summary of a survey by Freedom House notes that "in 1900, there were no states which could be judged as electoral democracies by the standard of universal suffrage for competitive multiparty elections. The

---

[1] Amartya Sen, "Democracy as a Universal Value," *Journal of Democracy*, 10, 1999, p. 3.
[2] Francis Fukuyama, *The End of History and the Last Man* (New York: The Free Press, 1992), p. 42.

1

United States, Britain, and a handful of other countries possessed the most democratic systems. . . . By the close of our century liberal and electoral democracies clearly predominate. . . . Electoral democracies now represent 120 of the 192 existing countries and constitute 62.5 percent of the world's population."[3]

Sen, Fukuyama, and the authors of the Freedom House Survey recognize, of course, that democracy is not yet universally practiced and that it is not without its detractors. And while there are encouraging signs in the Middle East and "orange revolution" in Ukraine, there are also reasons to worry whether democracy is really taking hold in Russia, for example, and China's economic boom perhaps suggests a viable "third way." Furthermore, based on the experience of the war in Iraq and subsequent democratization efforts there, some have questioned whether democracy should be exported as foreign policy and whether it is suited to some societies. Nevertheless, the outcome of the twentieth century was that democracy shifted from a governmental form in need of justification in light of competitor forms of government to the default position of political legitimacy.

But democracy is not simply a set of governmental institutions and popular elections. It is also a set of cultural values and a form of citizenship. Voting and the rule of law are necessary conditions for democracy but not sufficient. A robust democracy requires a culture that respects the dignity of individuals and the freedoms we associate with that respect; but it also requires citizens suited for participation in democratic decision making.

What is paradoxical is that with the advance of democratic institutions internationally, many have argued that in the United States our democratic culture is in a fragile, precarious condition. Jean Elshtain, in her book *Democracy on Trial*, put it bluntly: "American democracy is faltering." She sees "warning signs of exhaustion, cynicism, opportunism, and despair."[4] Clearly Elshtain is not referring to the condition of our governmental structures. Her concern is with the quality of democratic culture and the outlook of people who compose it.

---

[3] Freedom House, "Democracy's Century: A Survey of Global Political Change in the Twentieth Century," http://www.freedomhouse.org/reports/century.html.

[4] Jean Bethke Elshtain, *Democracy on Trial* (Basic Books: New York, 1995), p. 1.

It would be an interesting exercise to imagine what Alexis de Tocqueville would think about democracy in America if he should return today. Some of his earlier observations would prove to be prescient: the threat of individualism to a shared sense of the common good, for example, or the threat slavery and the treatment of indigenous populations posed for American democracy. But I suspect he would not introduce the book about his journey through America as confidently as he did in the 1830s. This is what he wrote then:

Among the novel objects that attracted my attention during my stay in the United States nothing struck me more forcibly than the general equality of condition among the people. I readily discovered the prodigious influence that this primary fact exercises on the whole course of society; it gives a peculiar direction to the public opinion and a peculiar tenor to the laws; it imparts new maxims to the governing authorities and peculiar habits to the governed. I soon perceived that the influence of this fact extends far beyond the political character and the laws of the country, and that it has no less effect on civil society than on the government; it creates opinions, gives birth to new sentiments, founds novel customs, and modifies whatever it does not produce. The more I advanced in the study of American society, the more I perceived that this equality of condition is the fundamental fact from which all others seem to be derived and the central point at which all my observations constantly terminated.[5]

Of course, the condition of equality that he was referring to was the absence of a governing aristocracy. And he was aware that equality was not extended to women, blacks, and indigenous peoples. What he would observe today is the extension of equality of condition to women, Native Americans, and African Americans, though these are still works in progress in some aspects of American life. However, he still might find reasons to doubt the general equality of condition in America. He might worry about the inequality of condition evident in the widening gap between the rich or reasonably well off and the poor – a gap that very nearly mirrors the fault line of race. This is certainly one of the most graphic and painful lessons of the devastation of New Orleans by Hurricane Katrina where the daily television images of poor black residents of that city crying out for help underscored

5 Alexis de Tocqueville, *Democracy in America*, vol. 1 (New York: Vintage Books, 1990), p. 3.

the extent of our racial and economic divide. He would find many people who believed that there is unequal access to the legislative processes and to the offices of power. Some would say that America has the best democracy money can buy. He would find poor young black men disproportionately represented on death row and young Native Americans disproportionately represented in suicide statistics and in drug rehabilitation clinics. He would find discrimination against Latinos, Asians, and Arabs. He would find a country polarized about the rights of fetuses and about whether gay and lesbian couples should be afforded equal recognition and protection through marriage. Across all of these lines of class, race, gender, ideology, sexual orientation, and national origin, he would find cynicism about government, disengagement from the political process, feelings of disenfranchisement, and deep doubts about the capacity of democratic institutions to support the aspirations of a pluralistic culture. He would hear a chorus of editorialists and social observers decrying the precarious condition of American democracy.

While we have acted out many of Tocqueville's deepest worries about democracy in America, it is arguable whether we are any longer Tocqueville's America in important respects; whether the virtues he observed then are the ones that can sustain us now. The differences between then and now are not merely the result of incremental developments over time. The challenge posed to democracy by the diversity of our country today is not just additively different from the challenge of religious differences or differences in European origin in the early nineteenth century. Some would argue that the sheer scope of diverse origins of citizens as well as the political claims of gender and sexuality seem to raise challenges different in kind, challenges about the political significance of diversity. In the vernacular of recent political theorists, it is the challenge to democracy of *difference*.[6] The expectations of assimilation, of America as the great melting pot, are no longer a presupposition for democratic culture. But if that is the case, can a democracy accommodate difference without undermining a shared sense of civic identity that seems essential to it? Jean Elshtain claims that America needs "a new social covenant," one that

[6] See Seyla Benhabib, *Democracy and Difference: Contesting the Boundaries of the Political* (Princeton: Princeton University Press, 1996).

can embrace both our differences and our shared identity. But there is substantial disagreement – both in theory and in politics – about what form that covenant should take. Is it a renewal of commitment to the values of Tocqueville's America – to shared religious traditions, community, family, and civic associations – or is it these values that stand in the way of a genuinely pluralistic democracy? Is it to be struck in terms of the liberal ideal of freedom from intrusion and coercion, allowing diverse people to choose their own ways of living?, In the way the political lines are drawn today – between social conservatives and liberals – either of these alternatives is the source of the other's disease. And this also contributes to democracy's precarious condition. So much of our politics is polarized around competing claims about who are the legitimate bearers of American democratic values. Who are the true patriots and who are the enemies of democracy? We find ourselves in a time when to disagree and to criticize is to hate America from one point of view or another.

Democracy is not newly precarious, however. Democracy's first flowering in sixth- and fifth-century BCE Athens was a tumultuous and relatively brief affair. In his exceptional study of Pericles, democracy's first citizen, Donald Kagan described democracy as "one of the rarest, most delicate and fragile flowers in the jungle of human experience."[7] In the ancient world, democracy existed in a jungle.[8] It was not just that the career of Athenian democracy coincided with the long and brutal Peloponnesian Wars. It was no abstract observation when Plato sarcastically described democracy as "a delightful form of government, anarchic and motley, assigning a kind of equality indiscriminately to equals and unequals alike."[9] The Athenian Assembly was not the idealized public space of reasoned discourse that some political theorists long for today. The citizens of Athens were swayed by self-interests and interests of tribe. They were persuaded by powerful rhetoric whether or not it was on the side of truth. They were fickle in their loyalties. And they executed Socrates.

---

7 Donald Kagan, *Pericles of Athens and the Birth of Democracy* (New York: The Free Press, 1991), p. 2.
8 See Mark Munn, *The School of History: Athens in the Age of Socrates* (Berkeley: University of California Press, 2000).
9 Plato, *The Republic*, in *The Collected Dialogues of Plato* (Princeton: Princeton University Press, 1971), R558c, p. 786.

The critics of classical democracy who were contemporary with it have been more influential to political theory than democracy's friends. Apart from Pericles' "Funeral Oration" as told by Thucydides, most of what we know of a positive sort about democratic theory in classical Greece we must glean from its critics.[10] Plato was clearly antidemocratic. (Whether Socrates was is a matter I will take up later.) In the *Statesman*, Plato has the Stranger tell the young Socrates that of all possible constitutions, "democracy is the worst so far as law abiding is concerned and the best for flouting the law."[11] The general line of this criticism was familiar before Plato, sufficiently familiar that Herodotus gave it prominence in his discussion of the three forms of government in his *Histories*. He put it in the mouth of an imagined Persian rebel leader:

[I]n a democracy, malpractices are bound to occur; in this case, however, corrupt dealings in government services lead not to private feuds, but to close personal associations, the men responsible for them putting their heads together and mutually supporting one another. And so it goes on, until somebody or other comes forward as the people's champion and breaks up the cliques which are out for their own interests. This wins him the admiration of the mob, and as a result he soon finds himself entrusted with absolute power – all of which is proof that the best form of government is monarchy.[12]

After Plato, Aristotle was to continue this criticism. Of the four types of democracy that he discussed, he identified extreme democracy, that is, democracy as practiced in Athens, to be the worst because "all offices are open to all, and the will of the people overrides all law."[13]

After the collapse of democracy in the ancient world, democracy was disparaged or ignored for much of the next two millennia. Even as recently as the eighteenth and nineteenth centuries – as the philosophical elements that we now take to be integral to modern democracy were being shaped – the term *democracy* was typically used either

---

[10] See A. H. M. Jones, *Athenian Democracy* (Baltimore: The Johns Hopkins University, 1986), pp. 41–72.
[11] *The Statesman*, in *The Collected Dialogues of Plato*, 303b, p. 1074.
[12] *Herodotus: The Histories*, Aubrey de Selincourt, trans. (New York: Penguin Books, 1954), p. 187.
[13] Aristotle, *The Politics*, in *The Basic Works of Aristotle*, Richard McKeon, trans. (New York: Random House, 1966), IV4, p. 1119.

narrowly to designate the political regime of Athens or as a term of abuse, naming a form of government that leads inevitably to lawlessness and anarchy.[14] And when it was used in a less hostile way, it was not intended to designate a governmental form to which we should or could aspire. Rousseau famously declared that "if there were a people of gods, it would govern itself democratically. Such a perfect government is not suited to men."[15] The flip side of this coin was James Madison's claim, in the *Federalist Papers*, that "had every Athenian citizen been born a Socrates: every Athenian assembly would still have been a mob."[16]

These views are not so far apart as they might seem. What Rousseau's observation implied is that the success of a democracy, ideally realized, requires a god-like capacity to transcend the personal and partial perspective in favor of the common good. Madison's view was based on democracy in practice. He shared the views of Plato and Aristotle that it is the "confusion and intemperance of the multitude"[17] that is democracy's major failing.

From our perspective in the heyday of democracy, we forget that the Founding Fathers did not originally understand themselves to be founding a democracy. Joseph Ellis reminds us that Thomas Jefferson, with whom we so often identify the democratic intentions of the American Revolution, rarely used the term *democracy* and when he began to, after his election as President of the United States in 1800, he used it interchangeably with *pure republicanism*. When he was called a *democrat* by the Federalists it was a term of derision.[18] And when Jefferson came to use democracy with approval, it was because of his dismay over how far government had strayed from the true revolutionary spirit of 1776. For Jefferson, democracy or pure republicanism called for the return to the essence of that revolution – freedom from tyranny, citizens'

---

[14] See Pierre Rosanvallon, "The History of the Word 'Democracy' in France," *The Journal of Democracy*, 4, 1995, pp. 140–54.

[15] Jean-Jacques Rousseau, *On the Social Contract*, Roger D. Masters, ed. and Judith R. Masters, trans. (New York: St Martin's Press, 1978), p. 85.

[16] Alexander Hamilton, James Madison, and John Jay, *The Federalist Papers* (New York: Bantam Books, 1983), p. 281.

[17] *Federalist Papers*, p. 281.

[18] Joseph J. Ellis, *American Sphinx: The Character of Thomas Jefferson* (New York: Alfred A. Knopf, 1997), pp. 170–1.

voluntary consent to government, distrust of centralized government that favored more local forms of participation, simplicity, and agrarian ways of life and values and so forth.[19]

Despite Jefferson's use of the terms *democracy* and *republicanism* interchangeably, they were more commonly seen as competing visions and it was the republican vision that was intended by most of the Founders. Gordon Wood, in his exceptional book, *The Radicalness of the American Revolution*, details how the republican aims of the American Revolution, to the dismay of many of the Founders, gave way to democracy. According to Wood, "the irony of the Revolution was that it sought to create a society and government established on republican principle. . . . They sought to construct a society and government based on virtue and disinterested pubic leadership and to set in motion a moral movement that would eventually be felt around the globe."[20] What the Revolution created instead was a democratic society of competitive individualists. Wood writes: "Well before 1810 many of the founding fathers and others, including most of the older leaders of the Federalist Party, were wringing their hands over what the Revolution had created and most American citizens were celebrating: American Democracy."[21]

The purpose of these historical reminders about democracy is to suggest that democracy is not newly precarious. It always has been. Its precariousness is owed to its historical contest with other candidates for legitimacy. But it is also owed to the tendencies internal to the nature of democratic culture, tendencies that its critics have been concerned about all along, tendencies toward the dissolution of the common good, and toward anarchy and disorder. I will be arguing that precariousness is not a merely contingent, circumstantial feature of democracy's career. Rather, it is an aspect of the nature of democratic culture and how democracy sits in the field of politics, and of tendencies inherent in democracy that pull against one another in ways that always put it at risk. As such, it places unusual demands on citizenship, demands not captured when we only think of citizenship in terms of rights that

---

[19] See *American Sphinx*, pp. 260–1. See also, Garrett Ward Sheldon, *The Political Philosophy of Thomas Jefferson* (Baltimore: The Johns Hopkins University Press, 1991), pp. 141–7.
[20] Gordon S. Wood, *The Radicalism of the American Revolution* (New York: Vintage Books, 1993), p. 229.
[21] *The Radicalism of the American Revolution*, p. 230.

citizens in democratic society have or in terms of citizen participation as voters.

Fundamental disagreement about what democracy amounts to also contributes to its precariousness. To use the phrase William Connolly borrowed from W. B. Gallie, democracy is an essentially contested concept.[22] The contested nature of the concept is not merely academic nor is it recent. It has been with us from the earliest days of the Republic, with fundamental disagreement about the true meaning of the American Revolution. Many of the diagnoses of the current condition of American democracy trace it back to that debate and to the consequences of the version of democracy that prevailed over the republican vision. Michael Sandel's *Democracy's Discontent*, for example, argues that in the American experiment with democracy, republicanism was the path not taken and that the other path, liberal democracy, is the source of the malaise of public life in America. I will return to his diagnosis frequently in this book. It is philosophically and historically rich and Sandel is an unusually compelling representative of one side of the debate in political theory – and the culture more generally – between liberalism and what has variously been characterized as republicanism or communitarianism. Common to the republicanism perspective and communitarianism is the conviction that what is wrong with American democracy is liberalism.

The coupling of liberalism and democracy, an alliance so natural to us now, was not naturally allied through much of the history of liberal political theory or in the history of democracy either. The origins of the liberal tradition were not consciously within the context of a democratic conception. Liberal theories from John Locke to John Stuart Mill shared the historic worry about disorder and the tyranny of the many that were so often associated with democracy. It is worth remembering that the rise of modern liberalism preceded the reemergence of democracy. John Dryzek reminds us that "it is only in the twentieth century that liberalism and democracy really reached an accommodation, such that 'liberal democracy' could fall easily from the lips."[23] Even

---

[22] W. B. Gallie, "Essentially Contested Concepts," *Proceedings of the Aristotelian Society*, 56, 1955–6, pp. 167–98 and William E. Connolly, *The Terms of Political Discourse* (Princeton: Princeton University Press, 1974).

[23] John S. Dryzek, *Deliberative Democracy and Beyond: Liberals, Critics, Contestations* (Oxford: Oxford University Press, 2002), p. 9.

in the twentieth century, the alliance between liberalism and democracy has been uneasy. "Like many marriage partners, liberalism and democracy are totally incompatible, yet cannot live apart," is the way Alan Wolfe has put it.[24] Liberalism brought to the marriage the centrality of individual freedom, and democracy brought political equality. The two have struggled with one another ever since, and democrats who are not liberals – communitarians such as Michael Sandel, for example – have struggled to break them up, to save democracy from the mischief of its partner.

The disagreement between liberalism and communitarianism that matters to me is their differing views about the nature of democratic citizenship. For liberalism, the center of gravity of citizenship is rights citizens are assured through the rule of law, and crucially the right to vote. Judith Shaklar, in her book *American Citizenship*, examines what it is that was being demanded by women and descendents of African slaves in their quest for citizenship and uses this analysis to identify what she takes to be central. While she acknowledges other meanings of citizenship, she identifies social standing as the core, the marks of which are inclusion in the polity through voting, and the absence of barriers to work and earn. On her view, citizenship is characterized not by qualities that citizens possess but by the guarantee of their equal opportunities.[25] In contrast, communitarians focus on the civic virtues citizens need to sustain self-governance. Michael Sandel, for example, writes that "[m]ore than a legal condition, citizenship requires certain habits and dispositions, a concern for the whole, an orientation to the common good."[26] And according to Sandel, these habits and dispositions are cultivated through attachments to community, family, religion, and associational memberships that orient citizens to shared common values and common interests. I think, however, that there is more to democratic citizenship than what either Shaklar or Sandel convey. The reason is that there is more to democracy than what either liberalism or communitarianism implies. Democracy is more than rights

[24] Alan Wolfe, *The Limits of Legitimacy: Political Contradictions in Contemporary Capitalism* (New York: The Free Press, 1977), p. 7.
[25] Judith N. Shaklar, *American Citizenship: The Quest for Inclusion* (Cambridge, MA: Harvard University Press, 1991).
[26] Michael J. Sandel, *Democracy's Discontent: America in Search of a Public Philosophy* (Cambridge, MA: Harvard University Press, 1996), p. 117.

and voting and different from civic attachments, though each of these is important. Exactly what more and how different are captured by what has come to be called *deliberative democracy*, a view of democracy different from both liberalism and communitarianism. I will be referring to the deliberative turn in democratic theorizing throughout this book, considering how it differs from liberalism and communitarianism, and suggesting its advantages over them for reinvigorating democratic culture. Deliberative theories of democracy place the weight of democracy on authentic participation in the process of achieving consensus about collective interests. For liberalism, the legitimacy of democratic consensus is guaranteed by the ballot – by citizens voting their interests. For deliberative theories, it is the legitimacy of the consensus-forming process that conveys legitimacy to voting. For deliberative democrats, communitarians overestimate the role of common values, especially for a pluralistic democracy such as ours, and therefore underestimate how deliberation among diverse citizens shapes common interests rather than responds to them. In the course of this book I will be urging the deliberative approach to democratic theory, but my goal is not to extend deliberative theorizing. Rather, I want to consider what it demands of democratic citizenship. For the most part, deliberative theorists have focused on the inadequacy of liberal and communitarian theories for a pluralistic democracy and on the conditions for authentic deliberation. My aim is to draw out the implications of what democratic deliberation requires of citizens and to suggest why this view of citizenship is essential for a vibrant democracy.

In Chapter 1, I will consider the condition of democratic culture in the new century. I will focus on the cynicism and distrust that seem endemic, at least as they are represented in opinion surveys and by editorialists. I will explore several diagnoses of the current condition of democracy that trace it to the excesses of liberal individualism. I do so with two purposes in mind. First, I want to disentangle various claims about the nature of cynicism and distrust in American culture to consider in what senses they are destructive of democracy and why. Second, I want to extract from the tangle a sense of distrust that was central to the origins of liberalism. I will argue throughout the course of the book that this aspect of liberalism remains vital to democracy even if other aspects are problematic.

In Chapter 2, I will begin to make that case for thinking about democracy in deliberative terms. It will grow out of the claim that doubt and democracy are made for one another. I will distinguish three kinds of doubt and explore their relationship to democracy and to the demands they set for democratic citizenship. Democratic politics is constituted by uncertainty and the contingency of social existence. It is because there is disagreement, often of a fundamental nature, about collective interests and common goods that the people are expected to participate in decisions that affect them all. If there was certainty in the affairs of citizens, one would not want democratic decision making, one would want the philosopher-king. However, disagreement about the collective good is a persistent feature of the political. In a democracy collective agreements are always provisional, always open for refashioning. In this sense, democracy is not so much a set of institutions as it is a collectively critical process of consensus formation. But it is a process that is constitutively incomplete. Uncertainty and doubt constitute the epistemic field, so to speak, of democratic citizenship.

Another form of doubt grows out of tensions inherent in democratic culture: tensions between equality and liberty, in the boundaries between public and private life, in the conflict between the desire for individuality and the conformist tendencies of society, and in the dynamics of inclusion and exclusions in a pluralist democracy. The always present capacity within a democracy for one aspect of these tensions to overwhelm the other requires wariness, vigilance, and dissent as a permanent aspect of democratic citizenship. Finally, democratic deliberation requires the capacity for self-doubt. I will call this capacity *deep doubt* because it requires that citizens in a democracy have both resolute convictions about things that matter and also a willingness to revisit and revise those convictions through participation with others in decisions about collective interests.

My interest, then, will not be with democratic theory but rather with the democratic personality. The role of doubt in democracy places significant demands on what it is to be a citizen in a democracy. Too often we associate citizenship with either the rights individuals are guaranteed by democratic government, or the opportunities afforded to individuals to participate in self-rule. Insufficient attention is given to, for lack of a better phrase, the traits of character that are necessary for democratic participation, given democracy's constitutive uncertainty.

Chapters 3, 4, and 5 will be historical case studies of Socrates, Montaigne, and Rousseau, respectively. They are intended to focus on characteristics of individuals that I will claim are necessary for democratic citizenship. They will illustrate deep doubt but also they will cast light on contemporary issues about the quality of democratic culture today. I need to say something now about why I undertake these historical studies. One reason, of course, is that they provide a certain distance from the intensity and immediacy of our own debates, allowing a somewhat more sober analysis than is sometimes possible with controversies so close at hand. Another reason is that they illustrate how people in other times thought differently than we do about fundamental matters and thus how we might think differently. But my strategy is not to recover these historical positions to place them beside contemporary ones. Historical recovery in any pure sense is not possible. Also, merely placing the past next to the present would at best allow some comparisons and contrasts, but would not motivate the refashioning of contemporary issues in the way that I think we need to refashion them if we are to get beyond certain polarizing and bifurcating tendencies of current political controversies. So I want to structure engagements between present controversies and historical figures, going to their positions with our issues in mind, and returning to our issues on the basis of rethinking their positions. I think this will provide fresh readings of important figures, but more important, it will allow fresh thinking about democratic possibilities.

But why Socrates, Montaigne, and Rousseau? They share two features that are central to how I think about democracy and its problems. First, doubt figures centrally in their positions, and what I want to argue in this book is that doubt and democracy are joined in ways that are essential to a vibrant democratic culture. Second, each of them has been interpreted by reasonable and serious scholars in diametrically opposing ways on issues that are central to current discussions about the condition of democratic culture. Socrates has sometimes been taken to be the arch enemy of democracy, and through his trial and death, as a martyr to the dangers of rule by the majority. This is not an unreasonable view and it has been articulated by both friends and enemies of democracy and by those who believe that Socrates is a saint and those who believe him to have been disingenuous and irresponsible. But equally reasonable people have held Socrates up as the exemplar of democratic citizenship. In a similar way, Montaigne has been interpreted as both an apologist for orthodoxy and the status quo and also as the father of liberalism, advocate for the dignity of the individual, and champion of the revolutionary capacity of critique in the face of traditional authority. Rousseau has been interpreted by some as the theorist of freedom, self-determination, and authenticity and by others as the advocate for a totalitarian democratic society in which the general will, not the individual, is absolute.

When we ask how it is that reasonable scholars could have such conflicting interpretations at such fundamental levels, the easy answers lay the contradictions at the doors of Socrates, Montaigne, and Rousseau. Socrates' famous irony and Plato's attempt to place his former teacher in the best possible light are the source of the interpretive problem, some would say. Montaigne changed his view over time and had not bothered to make his earlier essays consistent with his later essays. Rousseau simply contradicts himself. But this is much too simple. It invites another question. How could otherwise brilliant, insightful, and influential philosophers be inconsistent at so basic a level as to whether they were for or against democracy, the status quo, or individual freedom? There must be something else going on, something that is missed in these either/or interpretations and missed in conclusions about disingenuousness, inconsistency, and contradiction.

I will approach these case studies on the basis of a principle of interpretive charity. I will assume that smart philosophers are capable of recognizing inconsistencies in their thinking and that they seek to articulate coherent, consistent views. So I will assume consistency unless the interpretive price becomes just too high. But there is more to it than interpretive charity, as my goal in these historical studies of Socrates, Montaigne, and Rousseau is not "to get them right." My goal is to show how the attempt to get them right reveals a complexity and subtlety in the issues that concern them that can cast light on our own thinking about democracy and its problem. I want to bring some of their complexity and subtlety into our thinking, which is too often structured as choices between mutually exclusive positions. Thinking our way through some recent political issues and political disagreements is not easy in a culture that structures them as confrontations between right and left, red states and blue states, choices between mutually exclusive standpoints, debates over who does and who does not respect life and cherish the family, or charges about who are un-American and who are patriots.

Finally in Chapter 6, I will consider democratic education. From the beginning of the Republic, democracy and education have been intertwined. Many of the Founders championed education at public expense because they believed that through education the artificial, inherited aristocracy would be replaced with a society based on ability and merit. They also believed that education was essential for demo-cratic citizenship, that educated citizens would be able to transcend private and partial interests in favor of the good of all. In our own day, when democracy seems so much at risk, education can be a venue for reinvigorating democratic possibilities. I will primarily be concerned with higher education, but some of what I will be discussing is rele-vant to education generally in a democracy society. I will explore four connected questions. Who has legitimate authority to say what demo-cratic education is? In a democracy, control of the content of education must be democratic. How might educational institutions model demo-cratic processes? What roles should educational institutions serve in a democracy? And finally, how do we educate students for the demands of democratic citizenship, especially given democracy's uncertainty and constitutive incompleteness? This last question presupposes the view of democratic citizenship that I argue for in the course of this book, a view of citizenship that accepts, even embraces, the uncer-tainty that is part of democracy's condition and that appreciates the role doubt must play in the face of undemocratic tendencies inher-ent in democratic culture. Alan Keenan has argued that democracy requires a conception of citizenship that affirms rather than denies "democracy's constitutive incompletion, such a mode of democracy would require attitudes of forbearance, self-limitation, and openness to collective self-questioning."[27] I will consider how we might educate students for these attitudes.

[27] Alan Keenan, *Democracy in Question: Democratic Openness in a Time of Political Closure* (Palo Alto, CA: Stanford University Press, 2003), p. 15.

1

Distrust, Cynicism, and Indifference

> I worry no matter how cynical you become, it's never enough to keep up.[1]
>
> Judy Wagner, *In Search of Signs of Intelligent Life in the Universe*

It has become commonplace for editorialists and social observers to despair over the degree to which Americans have become cynical about politics and public institutions. On the second day of the new century, nationally syndicated editorialist David Broder, for example, worried that "the reputation of elected officials in general – and of legislative bodies in particular – has rarely been lower than it is today . . . more Americans say they cannot trust the people they elect to look out for the national interest – or even to represent the views of those who chose them."[2] Political philosopher Michael Sandel, for another example, introduces his widely discussed book, *Democracy's Discontent*, by observing that "at a time when democratic ideals seem ascendant abroad, there is reason to wonder whether we have lost possession of them at home. Our public life is rife with discontent. Americans do not believe they have much say in how they are governed and do not trust

---

[1] Judy Wagner, *The Search for Signs of Intelligent Life in the Universe* (New York: Harper and Row, 1986), p. 26.
[2] David Broder, "Historical Election Shaping Up," *The Buffalo News*, January 2, 2000, p. 3. This was a recurring theme in Broder's editorials for the *Washington Post*, *The Plain Dealer*, and other newspapers.

government to do the right thing."[3] The views of Sandel and Broder are shared by a great many political observers. They are supported by decades of opinion surveys tallying the pulse of the American people's disillusionment with government. The consequences of disillusionment and distrust are also evident: the smallest percentage of voter participation in national elections of any democratic nation – despite an occasional exception; an increasing reluctance of citizens to seek elective office; decrease in the number of young people entering public service careers; and a decline in civic participation and associational life generally.

This is not just an American phenomenon,[4] though the focus on political distrust and its consequences has been more intense in the United States. There is no point citing specific statistics and survey results because they will be replaced by still others in the years to come. As in the past, results will fluctuate in relation to changing circumstances. There was an uptick of confidence in government after the terrorists' destruction of the World Trade Center and a downturn following an unusually dismal economic forecast, for example, or following the disastrous response of government agencies to the destruction of Hurricane Katrina along the Gulf Coast of the United States. But the general trend has been established for decades and there is little reason to expect a significant change any time soon.

There has been a good deal to be disillusioned about lately: presidential dissimulation about sexual indiscretions; a presidential election held hostage to ballot irregularities and finally settled by the courts; terrorist attacks within the United States and persistent

---

[3] Michael J. Sandel, *Democracy's Discontent: America in Search of a Public Philosophy* (Cambridge, MA: Harvard University Press, 1996), p. 3. Subsequent references are to "DD" and page number in the text.

[4] See, for example, Pippa Norris, ed., *Critical Citizens: Global Support for Democratic Governance* (Oxford: Oxford University Press, 1999), which includes cross-national studies of industrial democracies as well as case studies of Sweden, Germany, and South Korea. See also Ole Borre, "Critical Issues and Political Alienation in Denmark," *Scandinavian Political Studies*, 23, 2000, pp. 385–410; Geoff Dow, "Beyond Cynicism and Desperation," *Australian Journal of International Affairs*, 56, 2002, pp. 39–46; John F. Cooper, "Taiwan: Democracy Gone Awry?," *Journal of Contemporary China*, 12, 2003, pp. 145–63; and Leif Utne, "Don't Cry for Argentina," *Utne Reader*, January–February 2003, pp. 17–19.

questions about what was known in advance and by whom and how
seriously it was taken; the U.S. invasion of Iraq and serious doubts
about the intelligence information on which it was justified; corporate corruption of disastrous proportions and its political ramifica-
tion; increasingly negative and nasty political campaigns at all levels;
and inept governmental response to natural disasters – just to name a
few that ushered in the new century.

There has been considerable finger pointing at who may be responsible for fostering this culture of distrust. Some point in the direction
of the news media, citing journalists' penchant for covering politics
and policy deliberation in terms of the "game" of politics instead of
the substantive issues at stake. The irony was completely lost on a CNN
reporter recently who, when interviewing a colleague reporter about
charges that documents about President Bush's National Guard service
were forgeries, concluded their several minute discussion by asking:
"When are the presidential candidates going to talk about health insurance instead of these charges?" In their book, *Spiral of Cynicism,* Joseph
Cappella and Kathleen Jamieson have argued that the dominant tendency of political reporting that frames politics in terms of winners and
losers, political strategies, and personal motives has had a direct impact
on the level of public cynicism about politics, political campaigns, government generally, and the quality of policy debates. During the most
recent presidential campaign, Chris Matthews – among the most popular political commentators on television – unself-consciously called his
program "The Horse Race." It is an open question, however, whether
cynical news coverage causes public cynicism or merely reflects what
politics has become. Cappella and Jamieson are cautious about making claims of cause and effect. But they do claim that there has been a
circular and self-destructive relationship created between cynical news
coverage, politicians, and the public. If reporters believe that political
discourse is motivated more by "spin" than substance, they are more
likely to report it in terms of strategy. If political leaders believe that
the press only responds to the game of politics, they are more likely
to frame their discussion of issues that way. The press and politicians
each justify themselves in terms of what they believe are the other's
expectations. And both the press and politicians think they are merely
giving the public what it wants. They perceive the public as more interested in the horse race than the substance of politics. Thus the spiral

of cynicism. Regardless of who caused what, cynicism now seems to be systemic.[5]

Journalists have argued something similar. James Fallows, while editor of *U.S. News & World Reports,* observed that "by choosing to present public life as a contest between scheming political leaders, all of whom the public should view with suspicion, the news media help bring about that very result."[6] He continues, "[A] relentless emphasis on the cynical game of politics threatens public life itself, by implying day after day that the political sphere is mainly a struggle for domination, rather than a structure in which citizens can deal with worrisome collective problems."[7]

Given the entrenched pattern of distrust and cynicism, it is not at all clear whether or how it might be reversed. There have been a number of thoughtful proposals for how civic life and democratic participation might be reinvigorated and I will consider several of them in the course of this book. I think that there are more basic questions that need to be considered first, however. How much trust does democracy require? How much distrust can it withstand?

Clearly a successful democracy requires trust. For roughly Kantian reasons, we can agree that trust is a background condition for the possibility of social and political interactions. If we did not trust in the institution of banks, there could be no financial activity of banking at all, in the same way that if we could not, in general, trust in the judicial process it would make no sense to seek judicial redress when we think we have been aggrieved. We hold people accountable for breaches of trust – the senior officers at Enron, for example – because breaches of trust are deviations from our normal and justified expectations of the people who occupy leadership roles and offices. But how much trust is required for society to function, and in what must we trust?

Democracy is capable of withstanding quite a lot of distrust. We should not overstate the perilous condition of democracy today or the grounds for disillusion and distrust. American democracy has always been a raucous affair. Character politics did not begin with President

---

[5] Joseph N. Cappella and Kathleen Hall Jamieson, *Spiral of Cynicism: The Press and the Public Good* (Oxford: Oxford University Press, 1997), pp. 237–8.

[6] James Fallows, *Breaking the News: How the Media Undermine American Democracy* (New York: Random House, 1997), p. 7.

[7] *Breaking the News,* p. 31.

Clinton's sexual indiscretions. It has been – sometimes more, sometimes less – a part of presidential politics at least from the time of Jefferson's presidential campaign with journalists' allegations about his relationship with Sally Hemming. And President Bush's election is not the first to be settled outside of the hands of the electorate. Only the third presidential election in America's history – again Jefferson's election – was thrown into Congress for resolution. Jefferson, who was a contested candidate, presided over multiple tie votes and was only elected by a one vote margin through a combination of backroom politics and ballot irregularities. The legitimacy of Jefferson's election is still a matter of debate.[8] The earliest partisan and ideological divide in national politics was over the meaning of the American Revolution for the role of a federal government, and this debate centered on distrust of governmental power on the one hand, and distrust of the people to rule on the other. Unlike the cable news channels of today, the press in the early Republic made no pretense of being fair and balanced. As polarizing as the issues of the rights of fetuses or gay marriage is for us today, our so-called culture wars have not and are unlikely to divide the nation in civil war as did the abolitionists and apologists for slavery. Vice President Cheney's invitation, on the floor of the Senate, to a leader of the other party to "go fuck yourself," is at least no worse than Vice President Burr settling political scores with Alexander Hamilton with dueling pistols on the bank of the Hudson River. Despite it all, American democracy has survived, even flourished.

This is not to say that we don't face many urgent challenges. Racial, gender, and economic divisions run deep in our culture. We are polarized about moral issues and cultural values – about abortion, for example, or about the nature of the family and marriage. We worry about the influence of money and special interests on elections and policy decisions. The innocent are sometimes wrongly convicted and the guilty, especially the wealthy guilty, are sometimes set free. There is a disturbing trend toward corporate monopoly of media outlets and the quality of public discourse has been reduced to pundits from the left and right sneering and screeching at one another on television. Our need for increased security in the face of terrorism threatens individual

---

[8] See Bruce Ackerman and David Fontana, "How Jefferson Counted Himself In," *Atlantic Monthly*, March 2004, pp. 84–95.

rights. And so on. Doubt and distrust are not unreasonable attitudes in a democracy with serious problems and deep divisions.

Even in the face of the culture of cynicism that social observers so often depict, our democratic institutions seem secure and democratic processes seem to work well enough. Leaders get elected and administrations change in an orderly fashion, even when elections are contested. Laws get passed and rescinded and tested by courts. Highways get built and maintained. The press is, in general, free and the Internet has dramatically increased the diversity of sources of information. Basic rights are protected even as we debate their scope. Citizens are not prevented from voting even if some choose not to exercise their right to vote. We are free to associate and to worship as we please or not at all.

So in what ways are distrust and cynicism destructive of democracy? The short answer to this question is: It depends. It depends on what one means by *distrust* and what one means by *democracy*. I will turn to questions about the meaning of democracy toward the end of this chapter and in the Chapter 2. It is, of course, a debatable matter.

What distrust means is not so much debated as it is accepted as relatively obvious. The dominant tendency has been to use distrust, disillusionment, and cynicism interchangeably and to assume that all expressions of distrust are of a piece, and as such, that all expressions of distrust in government threaten democracy. There is an important difference, however, between being disillusioned about this or that president and being disillusioned about the Office of the Presidency in our democratic form of government. There is an important difference between distrusting the motives of particular legislators and distrusting the legislative process. The carelessness with which distrust, disillusionment, and cynicism are used serves to obscure what is so deeply problematic about some forms of distrust. But more important for my purposes, it obscures the important and legitimate role some forms of distrust play in democratic culture. What I intend to do in the remainder of this chapter is to distinguish different forms of distrust to consider why certain forms are destructive of democracy. In Chapter 2 I will argue that in important ways, other forms of distrust are essential for a vital democracy.

Political distrust is not the same thing as disagreeing with politicians, legislation, or courts' rulings or with being opposed to something that government does. Distrust is disagreement plus suspicion: suspicion about motives, intentions, influences, and uses of power. Suspicion about government is as old as the American experiment.[9] Almost from the beginning, the evolution of our form of government has been shadowed by movements that are suspicious about the very idea of government. This kind of suspicion is different from suspicion about the role and scope of government in that it is antigovernmental. It is the belief that, despite appearances to the contrary, government is evil: the belief that those who hold the reins of governmental power are engaged in a conspiracy aimed at robbing us of our freedom and securing their benefit. Conspiracy theory–based political movements are as old as the "Whiskey Rebellion" and as recent as the proliferation of patriot or militia organizations. They have been both right wing, such as the "posse comitatus groups" or neo-Nazi movements, and left wing, such as the Weather Underground and certain radical environmental or antiglobalization movements. It is worth noting that many political movements founded on a conspiratorial interpretation of government take themselves to be the true heirs of the American Revolution.[10] They ground their positions in the Founders' distrust of a too expansive government and too powerful political elites. They cite the Constitution and Bill of Rights. They point to expanding government encroachment and interference in our lives, to the existence of genuine conspiracies, and so forth.

What makes distrust of this sort dysfunctional is not just the fact that some of the alleged conspiracies are crazy: fluoridation as a Communist plot to weaken the resolve of American citizens, Area 54 cover-ups of alien invaders, government initiation of drug trafficking in black neighborhoods, and the satanic intentions of Proctor and Gamble, to mention just a few. And it is not that the belief that there are conspiracies engaged in by government and other public officials and institutions is unthinkable. One need only remember the FBI attempts to discredit civil rights leaders, the Tuskegee "experiments" with syphilis patients, Watergate, corporate cover-up of the health risks of asbestos

[9] See Garry Wills, *A Necessary Evil: A History of American Distrust of Government* (New York: Simon and Schuster, 1999).

[10] See Michael Barkun, "Violence in the Name of Democracy: Justifications for Separatism on the Radical Right," *Terrorism and Political Violence*, 14, 2002, pp. 193–208.

or tobacco, or the Archdiocese of Boston's cover-up and reassignment of pedophile priests. Conspiracy theories are not always unfounded or irrational. It is not unreasonable to distrust White House statements about weapons of mass destruction in Iraq and to suspect motivated dissimulation about the evidence upon which the invasion of Iraq was justified, for example, or to suspect collusion between oil interests and White House officials in developing environmental policy.

Some suspicions about government are well-founded, others are pathological. What distinguishes pathological suspicion from those that are well-founded, what distinguishes the U.S. Christian Posse Association's distrust of government from my own, is that their suspicion constitutes a closed lens through which all events are interpreted. Distrust of government provides the internal logic of their worldview. Their suspicion of government is, in some sense, like the faith of the true believer, walling off the belief and rendering it immune from doubt. For the conspiracy theorist, there is no evidence to the contrary, because the sense of conspiracy determines what evidence is. Their world tends to be divided between the forces of evil that must be resisted and defeated by forces of good; thus the possibility of violence is inherent in such a worldview.

By contrast, nonpathological distrust is particular in its suspicions and responsive to changing circumstances and new information.[11] It is part and parcel of participating in political processes involving people and power. And this is the point of beginning with conspiratorial distrust: to distinguish a form of distrust that is total in nature, which distrusts the very idea of government, from someone who distrusts the current administration or who believes that there was a conspiracy of legislative and corporate interests in formulating a particular piece of legislation.

Cynicism, like conspiracy, is also a generalized distrust. But it is generalized for different reasons and with a different result. It is relatively easy to see how conspiratorial distrust is dysfunctional because it so often leads to violence. It is less obvious why cynicism is dysfunctional.

---

[11] For a survey of the extensive psychological and social psychological literature on pathological distrust, see Roderick M. Kramer, "Paranoid Cognition in Social Systems: Thinking and Acting in the Shadow of Doubt," *Personality and Social Psychology Review,* 2, 1998, 251–75.

The dangers of cynicism are more subtle but no less a matter of deep concern. Whereas conspiratorial suspicion operates, in some sense, at the margins of democratic culture, some social theorists have argued that cynicism is deeply imbedded in the nature of democratic culture and that its danger is not that it leads to violence and revolt, but that it leads to disengagement. Disengagement serves to reinforce the very things about which one is cynical.

Consider two examples of this analysis. Jeffrey Goldfarb, in *The Cynical Society*, and Timothy Bewes, in *Cynicism and Postmodernity*, have each argued that cynicism is the inevitable outcome of the "dark underside" of democratic culture – at least democratic culture in the form that has come to dominate in the United States. For them it is more than a form of disillusionment with politics. Disengagement from politics is merely an instance of a more deeply rooted disengagement. In somewhat different ways, they trace the roots of cynicism to the individualistic, relativistic tendencies in democratic culture that cause us to lose confidence in our culture and its values, therefore viewing them cynically. Here is how Goldfarb makes the connections:

Cynicism has its philosophical basis in relativism. When we no longer know that our way of life is the best way, we learn to respect others, but we also begin to doubt ourselves. Our positions on political, social, and even religious issues come to appear accidental, more the product of who we are – our class position, national interest, and limited interests – than a product of how well we think and act. Thus the quality of what we say and do and what others say and do come to be understood cynically.[12]

Because this is anything but obvious and because it suggests a much deeper analysis of cynicism than the opinion surveys upon which editorialists rely, it is important to spend some time sorting it out.

Democracy, in the primary shape it has taken in America, is characterized by the joining of the democratic values of equality and self-governance with the classical liberal values of liberty and individual rights. Liberalism – in the classical sense that has roots in John Locke, Immanuel Kant, and John Stuart Mill, and in our own day represented best by the political theory of John Rawls – combines a concern to

---

[12] Jeffrey C. Goldfarb, *The Cynical Society: The Culture of Politics and the Politics of Culture in American Life* (Chicago: University of Chicago Press, 1991), p. 10. Subsequent references are to "CS" and page number in the text.

ensure political equality with a worry about the capacity government or the majority interest has to overwhelm the interests of individuals. In addition, liberal democrats are suspicious of older notions of the purpose of government and the state. They are suspicious of an idea – common to an older political tradition dating to the ancient Greeks – that the purpose of the state is to foster human nature or the best kind of life and the common good. They are suspicious of the idea that there is a knowable conception of the best life that could or should be fostered and they think that politics is defined by the ongoing contest over what the common good might be. Thus liberal democrats believe that the state should be neutral with respect to conceptions of the good life and they understand the role of government as providing a framework, in law and through governmental institutions, that assures fair procedures through which individuals are free to pursue their own conceptions of the good life in their own ways. Goldfarb believes that it is the centrality accorded to individuals in the pursuit of their own conception of the good life that leads to a culture of cynicism.

It should be clear that cynicism as Goldfarb understands it is a less casual, more philosophically specific concept than it is in ordinary usage. And it is also importantly different from the philosophical cynicism that had its origins in classical Greece. Cynicism in its ancient, original form – the form exemplified by Diogenes – was a form of social protest and criticism. Peter Sloterdijk, in his fascinating *Critique of Cynical Reason*,[13] has explored this form of cynicism and the ways it uses social satire politically. But modern cynicism, as it concerns social observers today, is something very different. It is not a critical or political strategy so much as it is alienated and politically impotent. It is not so much critical as it is merely mocking. More importantly, this merely mocking form of cynicism actually serves to aid and abet the most destructive aspects of democratic culture. Goldfarb summarizes the point this way: "Cynicism promotes acceptance of the existing order of things. . . . Cynicism supports and is a product of mass society. It makes economic, political, and cultural domination invisible, and casts serious doubts on cultural and political alternatives. *The substitution of cynicism for critical reason supports the mass-society underside of democracy*" (CS, 30). In a similar way, Bewes says that "cynicism appears in the

---

[13] Peter Sloterdijk, *Critique of Cynical Reason* (London: Vreso, 1988).

space left empty by mass culture's retreat from politics itself. Political engagement has no option, apparently, but to *be* cynical. . . ."[14]

This is a complicated charge. The relationships between liberal individualism, mass culture, cynicism, and political alienation are not obvious on their face. However, it is important to sort them out to appreciate how distinctive cynicism is by contrast with other forms of distrust and to appreciate how deeply problematic it is for a vital democratic culture. I will follow Goldfarb's account of the origin and nature of cynicism though I expect to depart from his view about how we might combat it.

In his analysis of the modern form of cynicism, Goldfarb takes his lead from Tocqueville's *Democracy in America*. Nearly every observer of contemporary American culture has been struck by Tocqueville's prophetic recognition, in the early nineteenth century, that individualism was both a cornerstone of American democracy and its potential undoing. Tocqueville coined the word *individualism*, but he was careful to distinguish between "individualism properly understood" and what he called "narrow individualism." The former he connected with those hallmark democratic virtues of liberty, independence, and self-reliance. In contrast, he identified narrow individualism with selfishness. Tocqueville's insight was his recognition of the capacity of the former to yield the latter.

Selfishness is a passionate and exaggerated love of self which leads a man to connect everything with himself and to prefer himself to everything in the world. Individualism is a mature and calm feeling, which disposes each member of the community to sever himself from the mass of his fellows and to draw apart with his family and his friends, so that after he has thus formed a little circle of his own, he willingly leaves society at large to itself. . . . Selfishness blights the germ of all virtue; individualism, at first only saps the virtues of public life; but in the long run it attacks and destroys all others and is at length absorbed into downright selfishness.[15]

Goldfarb's gloss on Tocqueville's account is this: "Democracy, as the rule of the people, requires reasoned autonomy of equal citizens. Individuals must be able to make up their own minds, make their own judgments. They must be free agents. But as free agents they

[14] Timothy Bewes, *Cynicism and Postmodernity* (London: Verso, 1997), p. 3.
[15] Alexis de Tocqueville, *Democracy in America*, vol. II (New York: Vintage Books, 1990), p. 98.

can become atomized egoists, disconnected from their traditions and fellow citizens and unconcerned with the common good" (CS, 18).

Many recent interpreters of American culture have focused on this same theme. Christopher Lasch has written about the "culture of narcissism" and he has analyzed how the psychologies of self-fulfillment and self-assertion have become survival strategies for some against the adversities of modern life.[16] The theme is echoed in many of the portraits of middle-class Americans in Robert Bellah and his associates' book, *Habits of the Heart.* Their case studies are intended to show how these strategies, undertaken as a way of achieving personal meaning, are ultimately self-defeating.[17] They are concerned about the increasing difficulty we have in expressing what matters most in anything other than the language of individual preferences. The connection between narrow individualism and the loss of a sense of meaning in life is echoed in the perspectives of medicine, psychiatry, and sociology in such books as *Pathologies of the Modern Self,*[18] which focuses on the increase in clinical incidences of a kind of malaise of meaningfulness in modern life. Philosophers, such as Alasdair MacIntyre[19] and Charles Taylor,[20] have traced the self-absorbed form of individualism to a dysfunctional moral system growing out of the Enlightenment, resulting in what Taylor refers to as a narrowing of our moral horizons. Social conservatives, such as Alan Bloom[21] and William Bennett,[22] connect individualism to cultural relativism, and they believe that cultural relativism leads to moral indifference, and ultimately, to a destruction of traditional American values. Bennett expresses this last point this way: "In living memory the chief threats to America Democracy have

---

[16] Christopher Lasch, *The Culture of Narcissism: American Life in an Age of Diminishing Expectations* (New York: W. W. Norton and Co., 1979) and *The Minimal Self: Psychic Survival in Troubled Times* (New York: W. W. Norton and Co., 1984).

[17] Robert N. Bellah, Richard Madsen, William M. Sullivan, Ann Swindler, and Steven M. Tipton, *Habits of the Heart: Individualism and Commitment in American Life* (Berkeley: University of California Press, 1985), p. 163.

[18] David Michel Levine, ed. *Pathologies of the Modern Self: Postmodern Studies on Narcissism, Schizophrenia, and Depression* (New York: New York University Press, 1987), p. 3.

[19] Alasdair MacIntyre, *After Virtue* (Notre Dame: University of Notre Dame Press, 1981).

[20] Charles Taylor, *The Ethics of Authenticity* (Cambridge, MA: Harvard University Press, 1992).

[21] Allan Bloom, *The Closing of the American Mind: How Higher Education Has Failed Democracy and Impoverished the Souls of Today's Students,* (New York: Simon and Schuster, 1987). Subsequent references are to "CAM" and page number in the text.

[22] William Bennett, *The De-valuing of America: The Fight for Our Culture and Our Children* (New York: Simon and Schuster, 1992).

come from without: first, Nazism and Japanese imperialism, and later, Soviet communism. But these wars, hot or cold, ended in spectacular American victories. The threats we now face are from within. They are far different, more difficult to detect, and more insidious: decadence, cynicism, and boredom."[23] Allen Bloom's book, *The Closing of the American Mind*, published nearly two decades ago, dramatized the linkage between individualism, relativism, and indifference, and while his analysis can be frustrating, it is not without insight.

It is still not clear why a book that was by turns densely academic and merely grumpy should have been a runaway best seller, but it was. I suspect it was the subtitle of Bloom's book, *How American Education Has Failed Democracy and Impoverished the Souls of Today's Students*, that caught many people's attention. Bloom's claim that relativism was at the root of the problems of our culture resonated with a growing nervousness about the way multiculturalism and the so-called culture wars were sweeping university campuses. The claim that the latter was responsible for the former – no matter how densely argued the support for the claim turned out to be – clearly resonated with enough of the book-buying public to place Bloom among the most financially successful philosophers in American history.

Though Bloom's book ranged from Plato's *Republic* to MTV and back again, his central point was rather straightforward: in the name of tolerance and openness, university professors are promulgating cultural relativism, and the consequence of cultural relativism among students is nihilistic indifference. Here is how Bloom put it:

Openness used to be a virtue that permitted us to seek the good by using reason. It now means accepting everything and denying reason's power. The unrestrained and thoughtless pursuit of openness, without recognizing the inherent political, social, or cultural problems of openness as the goal of nature, has rendered openness meaningless. Cultural relativism destroys both one's own and the good. (CAM, 38)

In the name of tolerance, in appreciation of other cultures, in an attempt to teach students to doubt dogma and question their own values, university professors actually teach students to value everything

[23] William J. Bennett, *The Death of Outrage: Bill Clinton and the Assault on American Ideals* (New York: The Free Press, 1998), p. 130.

equally, according to Bloom. That is, they teach students to value nothing any more than anything else; to value nothing in particular. That is how Bloom thinks American higher education has failed democracy. The result of openness and tolerance is an indifferent nihilism: an outlook that implies that anything is a good as anything else. "What is advertised as a great opening is a great closing" (CAM, 34). I will turn to education in Chapter 6. But for now I cite Bloom only to dramatize the claim that the root of the problem of American (democratic) culture is indifference, and that the sources of indifference are doubt and relativism.

While we might disagree with Bloom's analysis, we philosophy professors are all too familiar with the culture of indifference that he depicts, at least as it is expressed by some of our students. When the moral or political going gets tough in class, discussion is brought to a halt by a student's slight shrug of the shoulders and a dismissive "whatever." It doesn't really matter. Who's to say? Whatever.

Indifference, nihilism, and cynicism are simply different manifestations of the same cultural phenomena – disengagement and alienation.

Here, then, is the deeper logic of cynicism. Democracy's dark underside is the culture of individualism. As an individual, I strive for autonomy by making my own decisions, I pursue my own interests, and I seek my own fulfillment. In so doing, I call into question traditional and shared values. The values of my culture come to be seen as merely among the realm of possible values, and thus, they come to be seen as matters of historical accident and cultural preference. But this leads to the realization that even my own values are merely a matter of preference. Aided by the pedagogy of tolerance, I question the basis of my own beliefs and I come to believe that any values, my own included, are as good as any others. Which values really matter becomes a matter indifference. Indifference leads to a lack of personal conviction and I come to view my own and others' values, beliefs, and actions cynically.

As Martin Heidegger so tellingly put it: No one is willing to die for mere values.[24]

---

[24] Martin Heidegger, "The Question Concerning Technology," *The Question Concerning Technology and Other Essays* (New York: Garland Pub, 1977).

Based on this deeper analysis, the form of cynicism about politics that opinion surveys record and editorialists worry about is, at most, a symptom. Cynicism as Goldfarb understands it is more deeply disturbing than expecting the worst from politicians and distrusting this or that public institution. It is the outcome of a particular way in which democracy in America has evolved, resulting in a culture of indifference and disengagement when the moral and political going get tough.

Indifference is as much the enemy of democracy as intolerance. Indifference undermines our sense of conviction and resoluteness in areas of our lives that matter most. The policy issues that we face as a people – from foreign policy in the Middle East to restrictions on stem cell research – are, at root, conflicts about fundamental values. While I might be able to remain indifferent about other people's values, to some extent, in my personal dealings, to do so in the realm of public policy is tantamount to ceding the floor to the dogmatists and ideologues. This was Hannah Arendt's point in the third part of *The Origins of Totalitarianism.*[25] The seeds of totalitarianism are sown in the disaffected and indifferent mass. The true danger of cynicism, and the indifference that attends it, is that it undermines our sense of personal power to bring about change, reinforcing the status quo through our disengagement. The generality of cynicism – as contrasted with distrust of this or that politician or political process – is its total disengagement.

Paradoxically, then, cynicism serves to foster the very aspects of American culture that we would point to as the reasons why our cynicism seems reasonable. "Cynicism in our world," Goldfarb argues, "is a form of legitimation through disbelief" (CS, 1). What he means might better be phrased as legitimation through unbelief. Because of cynicism's seeming reasonableness, it diminishes our expectations for politics and public life, thus fueling the very conditions that give rise to it. It becomes self-fulfilling.

That cynicism in this sense characterizes many of our attitudes is certainly true. But I do not think that we should take Goldfarb's claims about the ubiquity of cynicism or Bloom's claim about the closing of the American mind at face value. Goldfarb seeks to persuade us

[25] Hannah Arendt, *The Origins of Totalitarianism* (New York: Harcourt, Brace and Jovanovich, 1973), pp. 311ff.

of cynicism's pervasiveness by connecting it with everything from the popularity of *USA Today* to the threat of totalitarianism. As for Bloom, I suspect that some of his observations about youth culture and the condition of the American mind were more ideological than analytically driven. And like a good many academics and journalists in 1980s, he blew up in-house disputes among humanities professors into a culture war, something that looks far less momentous from the perspective of the very real clash of cultures in the first years of the twenty-first century. Goldfarb and Bloom are right, however, that cynicism and indifference are politically debilitating.

No matter how compelling the analysis of cynicism's connection to the "dark underside" of democratic culture, claims about the pervasiveness of cynicism can conceal as much as they reveal. In the remainder of this chapter, I want to focus on two tendencies of the literature of cynicism that contribute to an important misunderstanding of public disaffection with politics in democratic culture. The first is the tendency of the survey research and its reporting by journalists to interpret all manifestations of distrust in politics and public institutions in the vocabulary of cynicism and its consequences. The second, closely related to this, is the assumption of some social theorists that distrust of government is necessarily destructive of democratic institutions.

Interpreting all manifestations of distrust in the vocabulary of cynicism leads to a misunderstanding about the place and meaning of distrust in democratic culture and to an overinterpretation of cynicism's presence. This, I think, is the general point of Vivien Hart's very interesting twenty-year-old study of political distrust in Britain and America. While the empirical aspects of her study are dated, the theoretical cautions that informed her work still apply.

Hart appreciated the existence of widespread disparagement of politics in Britain and America and understood why it should be a matter of concern. However, she questioned how various researchers had interpreted that disparagement. She questioned the degree to which their conclusions about public opinion were shaped by questionable assumptions that they took merely to be obvious.

Political distrust has been recorded and analysed under many labels: political cynicism, disenchantment, dysphoria, incivility, normlessness and scepticism to name a few. To add to the variety, a number of political studies of political powerlessness, inefficacy and futility identify the identical phenomenon or

a very close relation. The inventive terminology, however, conceals two crucial areas of agreement: in conceptual discussion, most authors relate their
favoured label to the root concepts of alienation or (sometimes and) anomie;
in their conclusions, most authors find these critical attitudes and their consequences harmful to democracy. Their prior assumptions, their particular
definitions and their facts combine to make this conclusion inevitable.[26]

Hart's research sought to understand the meaning distrust had for
those who disparage politics – its significance for them – rather than
simply recording its presence and assuming its cynical interpretation.
Furthermore, she challenged the conception of democracy that was
implied in the conclusion that political distrust undermines democratic institutions. To do so, she made a very important distinction:
between those who are alienated from and reject the norms of democratic society and those who distrust the current polity because of its
failure to live up to democratic norms. On the basis of this distinction,
Hart's research distinguishes between those who are alienated and
cynical and those who are distrustful. "If alienation is estrangement,
then it is the former group who are alienated, for their rejection is
permanent and profound; the rejection of the distrustful is temporary and remedial."[27] The distrustful – as opposed to the cynical – are
distrustful *because* they accept democratic norms. They are distrustful
because they experience a gap between those norms and their present
realization.

  Distrust construed as the gap between democratic norms and their
realization is the implicit backdrop of an interesting 1996 survey of
American political culture conducted by the Post-Modernity Project
at the University of Virginia in collaboration with the Gallup Organization. Again, the results are dated, but the conceptualization of the survey is highly relevant. This survey sought to understand *political culture*,
which its authors think is distinct from attitudes about politics that are
typically the subject of "trust surveys." The introduction to the survey
makes the distinction between political culture and attitudes about politics in this way: "[I]n public life, politics is to the weather what political
culture is to the overall climate. That is, if politics is the manipulation
of power, political culture is the normative context within which these

[26] Vivien Hart, *Distrust and Democracy: Political Distrust in Britain and America* (Cambridge:
  Cambridge University Press, 1978), p. 3.
[27] *Distrust and Democracy*, p. 30.

manipulations take place." It continues, "[T]he politics of a society may change and change a lot, but the normative context – the political culture – of a society will change only very slowly, and when it does so, its changes will be of great consequence."[28] Conducting a survey based on the distinction between political culture and politics, this research found relative stability in American's positive attitudes about ideals central to democratic culture – the climate of democracy – at the same time that the survey showed deep pessimism about politics and government.

This survey is revealing even to us now, regardless of how the exact percentages might have fluctuated over time. What it suggests is similar to what Hart's research suggests: It is against the background of commitment to democratic norms that distrust expresses itself. It arises from the gap – whether merely sensed or clearly articulated – between our trust in democratic norms and distrust of current political realities.

Now to turn to the second tendency of the cynicism literature, namely the assumption that distrust is necessarily destructive of democratic institutions. By variously characterizing the consequences of cynicism and, therefore, distrust generally, as alienation, estrangement, anomie, indifference, and impotency, it is easy to believe that the cure for what ails us as a culture is restoration of trust in politics and public institutions. This is the theme of Michael Sandel's *Democracy and Its Discontent*, quoted at the beginning of this chapter, and it is the theme of a veritable cottage industry[29] spawned by sociologist Robert Putnam's now classic study, *Bowling Alone*, about the dissolution of associational life and civic culture in America.

Putnam's study links the decline in political trust to a more general decline in what he and other social scientists have come to call "social capital" – that is, a decline in civic engagement, associational life, and social trust that were characteristic of an earlier time in American life. His research charts the decline, since midcentury, in the number of people participating in voluntary associations and community-based social networks. Putnam considerers a number of things that may

[28] *The State of Disunion: 1996 Survey of American Political Culture,* http://minerva.acc.Virginia.EDU/-postmod/survey_Home.html.
[29] See Theda Skocpol and Morris P. Fiorina, eds. *Civic Engagement in American Democracy* (Washington, DC: Brookings Institution Press, 1999).

have contributed to the decline in civic commitment and social trust, including changes in the American family structure, the consequences of racial integration, the expansion of government and the welfare state that crowds out private initiative in social areas, the increasing pressures of work (two-career families, single-parent households, etc), suburbanization including increased commuting and sprawl, the growth of electronic entertainment, as well as a decline in associational membership.[30] But the importance of his research is the connection he draws between the decline in civic commitment and social trust and a more general malaise about the quality of public institutions and our personal sense of well-being. "Social capital," Putnam claims, "turns out to have forceful, even quantifiable effects on many different aspects of our lives. What is at stake is not merely warm, cuddly feelings or frissons of community pride. [There is] hard evidence that our schools and neighborhoods don't work so well when community bonds slacken, that our economy, our democracy, and even our health and happiness depend on adequate stocks of social capital."[31] The causal link between this malaise with respect to politics and public institutions and civic disengagement, according to Putnam, works in both directions. It is as likely that the actual effectiveness of government and public institutions has declined because of the decline in social capital as it is the other way around. The important point is that they are inextricably linked.

Putnam's view has been as influential as it has been controversial. It has struck a nerve and spawned a cottage industry around restoring social trust and building social capital. It seems to me, however, that much of the concern expressed by Putnam and others about the decline in associational life and its consequences for democracy does not capture the deep cause of distrust in American life. I think it also overestimates the virtues of associational life, *per se*, in our past at the same time that it insufficiently appreciates the new forms that associational life has taken in the last few decades. Let me take the last point first. While membership in the Jaycees and Elks lodges is declining, it would be interesting to analyze the associational role played by, for

---

[30] Robert D. Putnam, *Bowling Alone: The Collapse and Revival of American Community* (New York: Simon and Schuster, 2000), pp. 277–84.
[31] *Bowling Alone*, pp. 27–8.

example, children's soccer leagues. While the "soccer mom" has been reduced to a voter demographic or a shorthand for stay-at-home moms whose role in life is to organize carpools and schedule dance lessons, I suspect that a closer analysis would show how informal organizations of parents around their children's sports programs tend to cross racial, class, and affinity lines and that Saturday morning games are as much a forum about what is happening in the schools and on the planning board as who will bring the Gatorade. I suspect that soccer leagues are a healthier form of associational life than fraternal organizations whose histories are those of homogeneity and exclusion. The exclusionary nature of the organizations that Putnam worries about is the point of Jason Kaufman's book, *For the Common Good? American Civic Life and the Golden Age of Fraternity*.

Kaufman analyzes the reasons why fraternal organizations flourished in the late nineteenth and early twentieth century and his conclusions should make one suspicious of the nostalgia for the golden age of voluntary organizations, fraternal associations, and interest groups. His thesis is that "the huge wave of organization building between the Civil War and World War I were motivated by the desire for exclusive social outlets that would allow individuals of different genders, races, ethnicities, and birthplaces to socialize in private, self-segregated groups."[32] He argues that American associationalism exacerbated racial, class, ideological, and religious differences by fostering homogeneity, exclusivity, and special interests. "That so many pundits should herald this American tradition as a model for the future I find deeply troubling," Kaufman writes.

At the expense of sounding dogmatic, I think the costs of the "golden age" greatly outweigh the benefits. Its most lasting legacies have been those very problems most lamented in America today: a long-standing tradition of racial prejudice and interethnic hostility; a pernicious political system dominated by special-interest groups; an ominous love for guns, accompanied by a menacing fear of government; a weak and subservient labor movement; and a half-hearted tradition of public social service provision, capped by repeated failure to pass even the most rudimentary universal health insurance legislation.[33]

---

[32] Jason Kaufman, *For the Common Good? American Civic Life and the Golden Age of Fraternity* (Oxford: Oxford University Press, 2002), p. 8.

[33] *For the Common Good?*, pp. 9–10.

I agree with Kaufman and am inclined to extend his dismay to the nostalgia for the communal bonds of towns and localities of an earlier day. I grew up in such a community in the 1950s and I suspect that it would rank toward the top on the indices of social capital formulated by Putnam and others. Neighbors knew and trusted neighbors. They brought casseroles when you were sick, checked up on the elderly, looked after one another's children, participated in the PTA whether they had children in the school or not, organized potluck dinners, supported the library, and supported recreation programs and teen clubs. They strolled together in the evening on the community pier. No one locked doors. There was so little crime that my father used to say people in the town had to take turns playing the town drunk. Citizens voted in impressive numbers on town issues and in state and national elections. Among the things they voted on and approved was a "sunset" ordinance that prohibited African Americans from being within the town limits after dark.

If unraveling community bonds of this sort is one of the causes of democracy's discontent, then I think it is discontent well worth having.

There are deeper diagnoses than Putnam's that nonetheless share Putnam's view about the place of civic associations in democratic culture. Michael Sandel's work responds to Putnam's same picture of malaise and discontent. But he traces it to two more basic concerns in American life: the fear "that we are losing control of the forces that govern our lives" and the sense that "the moral fabric of community is unraveling around us" (DD, 3). In seeking to get behind the malaise and understand its origin, he offers a compelling historical narrative that traces it to the loss of the civic republican beginnings of the American democratic experiment that he claims was brought about by the ascendance of a liberal democratic public philosophy. He believes democracy's discontent is the result of the public philosophy of liberalism that has been the dominate outlook for much of the twentieth century. He believes that the cure for democracy's discontent is to oppose liberalism and reclaim the path not taken, the path of civic republicanism.

Sandel's characterization of liberalism seems to me to be fair and right. "Its central idea is that government should be neutral toward the moral and religious views its citizens espouse. Since people disagree about the best way to live, government should not affirm in law any particular vision of the good life. Instead, it should provide a framework of rights that respects persons as free and independent selves capable of choosing their own values and ends. Since this liberalism asserts the priority of fair procedures over particular ends, the public life it informs might be called the procedural republic" (DD, 4). His central argument, however, is that the public philosophy of liberalism "lacks the civic resources to sustain self-government" (DD, 10) thus leading to our sense of a loss of control over our own lives and resulting in an erosion of civic community.

Sandel believes that the solution to democracy's discontent is to be found in reviving the older, rival republican tradition that was eclipsed by liberalism. For republicanism, self-governance requires more than what liberalism is able to underwrite. Political participation "means deliberating with fellow citizens about the common good and helping to shape the destiny of the political community. . . . It requires a knowledge of public affairs and also a sense of belonging, a concern for the whole, a moral bond with the community whose fate is at stake. To share in self-rule, therefore, requires that citizens possess, or come to acquire, certain qualities of character, or civic virtue" (DD, 6). According to Sandel, liberalism cannot provide these resources because it "conceives of persons as free and independent selves, unencumbered by moral or civic ties they have not chosen" (DD, 6).

While I am sympathetic to the emphasis Sandel places on the role of deliberation in reinvigorating democratic institutions, it seems to me that his way of framing the case against liberalism – in terms of its lack of civic resources – is importantly different from his essentially fair-minded definition of liberalism quoted in the preceding text. I shall argue in Chapter 5 that it does not follow that choosing one's ends entails being unencumbered by moral and civic ties. It should be remembered that liberalism arose out of a distrust of the *authority* of tradition *qua tradition*, and this is not the same thing as severing one's ties with traditional and civic resources. Severing one's ties in the sense that Sandel's criticism implies would be like attempting the impossible task of stepping outside of one's own skin, and I don't think that is what liberalism intends by freedom to choose one's own way of living. I anticipate this criticism of Sandel that I will offer later to make the point now that what is essential to liberalism is its distrust and critical stance toward tradition, not the metaphysical theory of the self, unencumbered or otherwise, that some liberals propose.

Liberalism evolved out of two oppositional stances: One was a distrust of the *authority* of tradition and the other was opposition to the view that there is a single common good or best way to live one's life. The liberal believes that our traditional, moral, and civic inheritance is sufficiently complex, disjointed, ambivalent, ambiguous, and diverse that it would be a perversion to think that one can discover in it alone "the common good." It also seems perverse to think that qualities of character and civic virtue are possible only in the context of an antecedently shared sense of "the common good" or to think that that formation of civic character is inconsistent with the idea of choosing one's ends. Civic character is a function of education – broadly considered – and educating people for informed participation in public affairs is as important to liberal public philosophy as it would be for republican public philosophy.

If republican public philosophy rests on the notion that tradition speaks with one voice or that a moral community can exist only on the basis of a shared sense of the common good then certainly its educational policy will be different. This has, of course, been at the heart of the political struggles for control over the schools, and was central to the so-called culture wars in colleges and universities in the 1980s. I will take up these issues in Chapter 6. Part of my argument there will be that the difference between a republican and a liberal conception of democratic education is the difference between education in pursuit of the common good and education aimed at providing the necessary disposition and resources for public deliberation given the fact of a plurality of views about ways of life and common goods. But republican disagreement with the *content* of a liberal's education is a far different claim than Sandel's claim that liberalism lacks the resources for character, civic virtue, and self-government.

For the liberal democrat, our community ties and civic associations are not so much found in our traditions as they are chosen by our sifting and sorting the inherited backgrounds of our lives. This was the point central to John Dewey, to John Rawls in his last writings, and to neopragmatists such as Richard Rorty.[34] One may disagree with Dewey, Rawls, and Rorty in their view that civic values and social

---

[34] See, for example, John Dewey, *The Later Works*, vol. 2 (Carbondale: Southern Illinois University Press, 1981); John Rawls, *Political Liberalism* (New York: Columbia

solidarity are made not found. But that is very different from the claim that their views are incapable of sustaining a robust conception of associational life and public commitment.

The point I wish to make now, however, is that casting the issue of America's discontent in terms of restoration of trust skirts the question, "Trust in what and to what extent?" and it obscures a much more fundamental disagreement about political activity and public life. It obscures the crucial role distrust must play in democratic culture. Cynicism and suspicion about democratic norms are deeply troubling. But distrust of politics and government may not be. The point is not only that gauging the current level of political distrust is not the same thing as gauging the level of political cynicism and alienation, it also suggests that commitment to democratic norms can withstand a great deal of political distrust and may even be strengthened by it. This should make us cautious about how we interpret public disaffection, but it should also cause us to think more carefully about the relationship between distrust and democracy. In what sense does democracy require trust? Trust in what? What sort of distrust is destructive of democratic values? Might distrust in some forms be essential for the preservation of democratic culture?

What I shall be arguing in the chapters that follow is that one of the ways to cure what ails us as a culture is to restore the quality of distrust. Let me begin to suggest what I mean by turning to Michael Oakeshott's posthumously published *The Politics of Faith and the Politics of Skepticism*.[35] In that manuscript Oakeshott focuses on an ambiguity, in modern European political thought, between the two styles of political activity stated in the title. His argument is that the ambiguity between the politics of faith and skepticism leads to ambivalence between thinking that government is an essential institution for the betterment of humankind, and thinking that it is at best a necessary evil.

The difference between the politics of faith and the politics of skepticism is not like the difference between two political theories – for

University Press, 1993); and Richard Rorty, *Achieving Our Country* (Cambridge, MA: Harvard University Press, 1998).
[35] Michael Oakeshott, *The Politics of Faith and the Politics of Scepticism*, Timothy Fuller, ed. (New Haven: Yale University Press, 1996). Subsequent references are to "PFPS" and page number in the text.

example, between liberalism and collectivism or between different conceptions of the authority of government. They are opposing styles, and though they are, in the abstract, opposites, he thinks it would be a mistake to think that one springs up in an opposition to the other or that what are abstract opposites are concretely antagonistic. He believes that "the history of modern politics (in respect of the activity of governing) is a *concordia discors* of these two styles . . ." (PFPS, 30).

According to the politics of faith, Oakeshott claims, "the activity of governing is understood to be in the service of the perfection of mankind" (PFPS, 23). This style of politics emerges, at the beginning of modern history, out of "a remarkable and intoxicating increase in human power" (PFPS, 24). It is not simply the view that government contributes to human improvement, it is the view that government is the primary contributor to the perfection of mankind, and it is the utopian view that it is toward perfection – not just improvement – that the politics of faith is directed. "[I]n this understanding of politics, the institutions of government will be interpreted, not as a means for getting things done or for allowing decisions of some sort to be made, but as a means for arriving at the 'truth', for excluding 'error' and for making the 'truth' prevail" (PFPS, 27).

By contrast, "the politics of scepticism (regarded as an abstract style of politics) may be said to have its roots either in the radical belief that human perfection is an illusion, or in the less radical belief that we know too little about the conditions of human perfection for it to be wise to concentrate our energies in a single direction by associating its pursuit with the activity of governing" (PFPS, 31). The politics of skepticism is based not on a doctrine of human nature – either perfectible or otherwise – but on a reading of human conduct. The activity of governing exists not as part of perfectibility but out of necessity because of the fact of human conflict. In so far as governing, in the political style of skepticism, is involved in improvement, it is not toward perfectibility of human beings, but toward improving the system of order and redress between individuals. That is, it is concerned with improving the system of rights, duties, and redress in the maintenance of order. Government is a necessary evil. And as such, "like garlic in cooking, government should be so discreetly used that only its absence is noticed" (PFPS, 36). I would add to Oakeshott's insight that even if one were a perfectionist about human nature, the skeptical style of political activity would not assume that government or public institutions are the places to achieve it. The emphasis would not be on perfecting government to perfect human nature, but on curbing its power to intrude in our lives and to demanding greater transparency and accountability of governmental institutions and offices. In the style of the politics of skepticism – and now I am going beyond Oakeshott's view – distrust is not a consequence of disillusionment with politics and public institutions or disillusionment about human conduct in the public space. Human beings and the public space are what they are, sometimes more so, sometime less. Distrust is the natural and essential outlook for the political style that is suspicious of those who would turn government to perfectionist ends. One would simply trust at one's peril.

We should remember, again, that the modern age was born of distrust – from Descartes's transformation of rationality into *critical* reason based on systematic doubt to the challenges to the tyranny of religious and political authority by Luther and Locke. Doubt about traditional beliefs and distrust of authority were the enemies of dogmatism and tyranny, the friends of enlightenment and progress. Doubt and distrust liberated science from superstition and individuals from subjugation.

While an interesting and complicated history could be written about the place of distrust in the origin of the democratic revolutions of the eighteenth and nineteenth centuries, it is the conceptual relationship between doubt, distrust, and democracy that interests me in the chapters that follow. For now, the need is to sharpen the distinction between distrust and cynicism.

Doubt, like cynicism, is born of distrust – distrust of authority based on tradition or force, or on unfounded opinion, or on the senses and passions as sources for knowing and so on. But it is distrust as a means: distrust in some things to achieve conviction about others. I chose the term *conviction* deliberately. It is the roles of doubt and *conviction* that I am interested in, not the epistemologist's concern about doubt and *certainty*. I will return to this issue in the Chapter 4.

Conspiratorial suspicion is aberrant and while it incites people to political action and even anarchistic violence, it will, I hope, always be marginal. Cynicism is distrust pure and simple. It is a form of doubt through which we lose confidence rather than gain conviction. Goldfarb's analysis focuses us on the loss of confidence. He thinks it is the result that follows from our recent questioning of American institutions in light of other cultures and values. To cite again what I quoted previously: "When we no longer know that our way of life is best, we learn to respect others, but we also learn to doubt ourselves. Our positions on political, social, and even religious issues come to appear accidental, more the product of who we are – our class position, nationality, and limited interests – than a product of how we think and act. Thus the quality of what we say and do come to be understood cynically" (CS, 10).

How very different is this from the style of doubt practiced by Socrates in the age of Athenian democracy or by Montaigne at the beginnings of the modern age. In the next chapters I will use both Socrates and Montaigne as case studies for a very different way of questioning and distrust. Let me anticipate the difference by contrasting Goldfarb's conclusion with that of Montaigne, expressed in his essay "Of Custom." It will illustrate the difference and suggest the direction I will be taking. In that essay, Montaigne surveys a wide and wild variety of beliefs and practices of regions and peoples very different from the French. The general thrust of the essay is to show the great variability in beliefs and to suggest that what one believes is merely a matter of custom and usage; that custom and usage can turn the most unusual beliefs into accepted practice. When we turn that suggestion to our own beliefs and values, what we recognize is that they too are the result of custom. As such, they are as groundless as any other. This is the sort of logic that Goldfarb thinks must necessarily lead to cynicism. But here is the conclusion that Montaigne draws: "Whoever wants to get rid of [the] violent prejudice of custom will find many things accepted with undoubting resolution, which have not support but in the hoary beard and the wrinkles of the usage that goes with them; but when this mask is torn off, and he refers things to truth and reason, he will feel his judgment as it were all upset, and *nevertheless restored to a much surer status.*"[36] That emphasis on the last phrase is mine. Recognition of the variability of custom and that our own customs are grounded not in truth but usage does not necessarily weaken

[36] Michel de Montaigne, "Of Custom, and Not Easily Changing an Accepted Law," *The Compete Works of Montaigne*, Donald M. Frame, trans. (Palo Alto, CA: Stanford University Press, 1965), pp. 84–5.

our conviction, Montaigne argues. It may even restore them to a surer status.

Montaigne found conviction in his recognition of the contingency of his cultural values, customs, and institutions. He found, through doubt, the capacity to live effectively in a tangled and uncertain world. By contrast, Goldfarb thinks that cynicism is the consequence of recognizing that our cultural values and institutions are groundless and relative. Goldfarb seeks an alternative to cynicism by finding an alternative to relativism. He seeks it in the "constitution of democratic values . . . readily observable in our history and in contemporary social, political, and cultural life . . ." (CS, 11). Fair enough. But when it comes to cashing in his alternative, it is more an exhortation for intellectuals to stop fostering cynicism and to reclaim democratic values as a framework in which people might reverse narrow individualism and the success of mass society. Pretty thin soup.

There are more compelling alternatives and I will consider two of them in the chapters that follow. Michael Sandel, whom I introduced to illustrate the growing concern about the condition of democracy in America, represents one such alternative. Sandel – like Goldfarb – believes that liberal individualism is the source of democracy's discontent, but he seeks to revive the tradition of republican civic virtue as a way of revitalizing public life and citizen participation in self-governance. His is a communitarian and republican alternative to liberal democracy. I will consider his view in greater detail in Chapters 3 and 4.

I will also be considering the "deliberative turn" in democratic theorizing[37] that has developed out of the critical theory of Jurgen Habermas. While I will be suggesting reasons why I think it is a compelling way of formulating a theory of democratic participation, my primary interest is to consider what it demands of individuals and what it

---

[37] Jurgen Habermas is generally identified as the source for the deliberative turn. See his *Communication and the Evolution of Society* (Boston: Beacon Press, 1979) and *Structural Transformation of the Public Sphere: An Inquiry into a Category of Bourgeois Society* (Cambridge, MA: MIT Press, 1989). See also Amy Gutmann and Denis Thomas, *Democracy and Disagreement* (Cambridge, MA: Harvard University Press, 1996); Seyla Benhabib, *Democracy and Difference: Contesting the Boundaries of the Political* (Princeton: Princeton University Press, 1996); and John S. Dryzek, *Deliberative Democracy and Beyond: Liberals, Critics, and Contestations* (Oxford: Oxford University Press, 2000).

suggests about a democratic personality and citizenship. A deliberative approach shares the republican concern about the impoverished condition of democracy and it shares the belief that liberal individualism is partly to blame. Deliberative democrats share the republican assumption that civic life is more extensive than electoral politics or governmental processes, the primary focus of liberalism. They assume a much richer and more variegated public sphere than liberalism, including civic and associational life but also extending to areas of common activity such as the workplace and schools. But they retain the core liberal value of respect for individuals and in particular the liberal assumption that a democratic culture is characterized by a plurality of values and diverse ways of life. But for liberal democracy, the ideal of self-governance is characterized in terms of voting through which citizens express their preferences, and by the rule of law upon which individual rights are protected. The deliberative turn shifts the center of gravity from voting as the expression of citizen interests to the processes of achieving reasoned agreement, processes that should be at work in a vital democratic culture in many more areas of our lives than government and electoral politics.

I will turn to a fuller discussion of what deliberative democracy requires of citizens in subsequent chapters. For now, I want to assert that while liberal individualism has been a source of cynicism and democratic discontent, there are aspects of the liberal heritage that are essential for a vital democratic culture, aspects that the republican alternative undervalues in its rejection of liberalism, but that the deliberative turn retains as essential.

2

Doubt and Democracy

The courage to doubt, on which American pluralism, federalism, and religious liberty are founded, is a special brand of courage, a more selfless brand of courage than the courage of orthodoxy: a brand that has been rarer and more precious in the history of the West then courage of the crusader.[1]

Daniel J. Boorstin, *Hidden History*

Doubt and democracy were made for each other, and this is one of democracy's central paradoxes. Doubt is joined to democracy's revolutionary origins. In ancient Athens and with its rebirth in eighteenth-century Europe and America, democracy was the consequence of questioning the legitimacy of the authority and power exercised over people against their will or without their participation. In this sense, doubt about the legitimacy of external authority was coupled with confidence in the people's capacity to govern themselves. However, democracy has embodied a continuing suspicion about that very capacity. Detractors and defenders of democracy alike recognized the people's vulnerability to the temptations of power, manipulation, and special interests through which the tyranny of the many merely supplants tyrannical monarchs. From the criticisms of Plato and Aristotle

---

[1] Daniel J. Boorstin, *Hidden History: Exploring Our Secret Past* (New York: Vintage Books, 1987), p. 183.

through the worries of America's Founding Fathers there has been fundamental doubt about the capacity of the *demos* for self-rule.

It is tempting to think that the revolutionary origins of democracy are of historical interest only, that doubt and democracy were merely linked at moments in time. It is tempting to think that doubts about our capacity for self-rule, legitimate though they may be, have been adequately tempered by the institutionalization of rights and the rule of law as protections against the tyranny of the many. In the first instance, doubt is considered to be merely coincidentally connected to democracy's origin. In the second instance, it is something we have overcome through the institution of democratic government founded on constitutional principles and the balance of powers. In neither case is it thought that doubt is in any way essential to democracy. But that is what I shall argue. I shall argue that doubt is integral to democracy in the sense that its absence would diminish democratic possibilities and risk democracy.

In developing this argument, I will consider three different but related dimensions in which doubt is essential to democracy. I will begin by considering how the revolutionary origins of democracy are integral to its continuing possibilities. Next, I will consider the place of doubt in relation to the internal dynamics of democratic culture. Finally, I will consider the connection between doubt and democratic citizenship. From these I will be deriving three modes of doubting that are essential for democratic citizenship: first, doubt as the epistemic field of democratic politics in the sense that uncertainty is the condition for the possibility of democratic politics; second, doubt as a generalized wariness and particularized dissent and resistance in the face of the undemocratic tendencies inherent in democracy; and third, what I shall refer to as deep doubt, a mode of doubt that I take to characterize democratic citizenship in a robust democracy.

Cornelius Castoriadis reminds us that democracy and philosophy "were born at the same time and in the same place."[2] He argues that this was not merely coincidental. The same impulse gave rise to both democracy and philosophy and it is essential to both. Castoriadis claims

[2] Cornelius Castoriadis, "The 'End of Philosophy'?" *Philosophy, Politics, Autonomy: Essays in Political Philosophy* (Oxford: Oxford University Press, 1991), p. 20. Subsequent quotations are to "PPA" and page number in the text.

that from the point of view of their origin, the singularity of classical Athens consists in being the first society in which questioning the
collective understanding of the world and of social life became possible, and in which choosing and judging between ways of representing
the world and ways in which society is constituted became thinkable.
In preclassical Greece, one's view of the world and social institutions
were given – given by the gods, through tradition, in the natural social
order. In a similar way, Castoriadis provocatively contends that the
idea of judging and choosing "would not and could not occur to a
Hindu, to a classical Hebrew, to a true Christian, or to a Moslem.
Classical Hebrews have nothing to choose." He continues, "[T]hey
have been given the truth and the Law once and for all by God, and if
they start judging and choosing about that, they are no longer Hebrew.
Likewise, Christians have nothing to judge or choose: they have to
believe and to love" (PPA, 87).

Whether or not one accepts Castoriadis's claims for the singularity
of classical Greece, he is right to draw attention to the radical nature
of the originating impulse of philosophy and democracy. No longer
merely inhabiting the given world and its social arrangements, the
activities of judging and choosing place them in our own hands to
be questioned and refashioned.

But Castoriadis claims that there is another aspect of classical Greece
that gave philosophy and democracy their distinctive shape. It was the
idea that at the root of the world chaos lurks. The idea of chaos was
central to the classical Greek vision of the world in two ways. First, chaos
referred to the void out of which the world emerged. Second, and more
important for giving shape to both philosophy and democracy, chaos –
in contrast to cosmos – referred to disorder that always lay below the
ordered surface of things, resisting the possibility of total ordering.
"This vision," Castoriadis claims, "conditions, so to speak, the creation
of philosophy. Philosophy, as the Greeks created and practiced it, is
possible because the world is not fully ordered. If it were, there would
not be any philosophy, but only one, final system of knowledge" (PPA,
104). Likewise, if the social world were fully ordered there would be

no field for political action and no sense in asking what the proper law is or what
justice is.... If a full and certain knowledge (*episteme*) of the human domain
were possible, politics would immediately come to an end, and democracy

would be both impossible and absurd: democracy implies that all citizens have the possibility of attaining a correct *doxa* and that nobody posses an *episteme* of things (PPA, 104).

Democratic politics is necessary because, in the realm of human affairs, certainty is not possible. If certainty was possible in human affairs, one would want the philosopher king. When those with power believe they possess certainty, one gets a tyrant. Democracy assumes, however, that collective interests are uncertain and contestable because no one has the truth of the matter.

I might add parenthetically that having been born together, the conceptions of philosophy and democracy that Castoriadis is describing are relatively short-lived. They die together. It can be argued that the death of Socrates marks the beginning of their mutual demise. Socrates was put to death by both Athens and Plato. Athens failed to recognize that Socrates was God's gift to democracy. Plato failed to recognize that Socrates's profession of ignorance was genuine and necessary for his philosophical way of life. I share Castoriadis's view that Plato's attempt to link certainty, virtue, and social order was a "philosophical monstrosity" so far as the Socratic outlook was concerned. I will return to this in the following text.

If democracy begins where certainty ends, to use Benjamin Barber's formulation,[3] what does this mean for how we understand democracy?

First, if democratic politics is constituted by uncertainty – if no one can legitimately claim to have *episteme* – then there is no privileged political position. This provides the rationale for the participatory nature of democratic decision making and the ideals of equal participation. If no citizen has a privileged position with respect to the good of all, then all citizens have an equally legitimate role in judging and choosing collective interests. This is why the democratic *polis* of classical Athens is characterized by the activity of discourse and why citizenship is characterized in terms of free and equal participation in the affairs of the *polis*.

There is an additional sense in which democracy and uncertainty are linked. Democracy cannot produce certainty. It can only produce the collective *doxa*, consensus in opinion. While democracy cannot

---

[3] Benjamin Barber, "Theory and Practice: Democracy and the Philosophers," *History Today*, 1994, p. 45.

produce certainty, it nonetheless must produce decisions. In this sense, democratic uncertainty is different from the more familiar doubts of the epistemological skeptics. The epistemological skeptic – the one who calls into question the foundations of knowledge or the possibility of certainty generally – can remain agnostic or suspend judgment. But in politics, citizens must judge, choose, and act. Benjamin Barber puts the difference this way:

This means that the political actor, unlike the speculative philosopher, can afford neither the luxury of agnosticism nor the Olympian nonchalance of skepticism. To be political is to *have* to choose – and, what is worse, to have to choose under the worst possible circumstances, when the grounds of choice are not given a priori or by fiat or by pure knowledge (*episteme*). To be political is thus to be free with a vengeance – to be free in the unwelcome sense of being without guiding standards or determining norms yet under the ineluctable pressure to act, and to act with deliberation and responsibility as well.[4]

Skeptical indifference is as opposed to democracy as the certainty of tyrants and true believers.

If democratic decisions are not made legitimate because they are certain, then in what does their legitimacy consist? It can only be in the legitimacy of the processes through which citizens deliberate together – under conditions of uncertainty – about what are common goods and collective interests. Decisions are made legitimate because citizens have an equal role in deliberating and deciding the collective *doxa*.

A second consequence of realizing that democracy begins where certainty ends is that democratic consensus is always provisional. In this sense, it is always open to question, challenge, and refashioning. Democracy should not be confused with the stable order of institution-alized forms that we identify with democratic government – rights, the rule of law, and so forth. That is not to say that these are not essential to democratic culture. They are. They are what prevent "government of the people, by the people, and for the people" – as Lincoln was to characterize democracy – from devolving into mob rule. Rather it is to say that democracy is the permanent possibility for contesting and refashioning institutions and the collective good. In this sense,

4 Benjamin Barber, *Strong Democracy: Participatory Politics for a New Age* (Berkeley: University of California Press, 1984), p. 121.

democracy is a process, not a destination. Democracy is forever open. Sheldon Wolin captures this, if somewhat cryptically, in the following way: "Democracy needs to be reconceived as something other than a form of government: as a mode of being that is conditioned by bitter experience, doomed to succeed only temporarily, but is a recurrent possibility as long as the memory of the political survives."[5] The memory of the political is the recognition that the political is permanently open and, thus, constitutively incomplete. Michael Walzer asserts something similar: "in democratic politics, all destinations are temporary. No citizen can ever claim to have persuaded his fellows once and for all."[6]

It is partly as a result of the open-endedness of democratic politics that from the collapses of democracy in the classical age to the drafting of the American Constitution so many have expressed doubts about the capacity of the *demos* to be trusted with self-rule. Under conditions of uncertainty and open-endedness, there is an inevitable craving for certainty and closure. The craving for closure invites either strong leaders, benevolent or otherwise, or collapses into the rule of the mob. Donald Kagan, in his influential studies of Pericles and Athenian democracy, has observed that "the paradox inherent in democracy is that it must create and depend on citizens who are free, autonomous, and self-reliant. Yet its success – its survival even – requires extraordinary leadership."[7] Pericles was more than simply the "first citizen of Athens." His leadership and the quality of Athenian democratic culture were joined, and after Pericles, Athenian democracy vacillated between tyrants and the mob. Many of the American Founding Fathers were as much concerned about the prospects of mob rule as they were about independence from British rule. Madison's claim that even if every Athenian citizen were a Socrates, the Assembly would still be a mob captured a fundamental uneasiness about the capabilities of the people to rule. Democratic culture seems to exit in the uncertain space between the tyranny of dictators and the tyranny of the many. Just as

---

[5] Sheldon S. Wolin, "Fugitive Democracy," in *Democracy and Difference: Contesting the Boundaries of the Political*, Seyla Benhabib, ed. (Princeton: Princeton University Press, 1996), p. 43.

[6] Michael Walzer, *Spheres of Justice* (London: Blackwell, 1983), p. 310.

[7] Donald Kagan, *Pericles of Athens and the Birth of Democracy* (New York: The Free Press, 1991), p. 9.

the ancient Greek world existed between cosmos and chaos, democracy exists between the craving for ordered certainty – whether of the tyrant or of the many – and the threat of dissolution into the anarchy of the mob. Alexis de Tocqueville also recognized something like this in his observations about democracy in France and America.

In his introduction to *Democracy in America*, Tocqueville was highly critical of the direction democracy was taking in France, his own country.

> In no country in Europe has the great social revolution that I have just described made such rapid progress as in France; but it has always advanced without guidance. The heads of the state have made no preparation for it, and it has advanced without their consent or without their knowledge. The most powerful, the most intelligent, and the most moral classes of the nation have never attempted to control it in order to guide it. Democracy has consequently been abandoned to its wild instincts.[8]

What are democracy's wild instincts? They are, I think, the familiar aspects of democratic culture that critics of democracy from Plato forward have fixed on – the *demos* devolving into the disordered rabble of individual interests or aggregated into a majority, replacing the tyranny of the monarch with the tyranny of the many.

In a somewhat obvious sense, tyranny and anarchy are the fundamentally undemocratic threats to democratic culture. Vittoria Bufacchi, in a brief but compelling paper, "Sceptical Democracy," argues that they are the opposing worldviews between which democracy is positioned. "The threat to democracy comes from two opposing extremes: from those who believe in the certainty of their beliefs (totalitarianism), and those who deny the existence of any truth (nihilism and post-modernity)."[9] Assuming something like the view of uncertainty and democracy I sketched in the preceding text, Bufacchi suggests that it is democratic decision making in the face of uncertain democratic skepticism that both characterizes the precarious position of democracy between these threats and enables its resistance to them. It seems to me, however, that tyranny and anarchy are not so much threats external to and challenging democratic culture, but rather, they are

[8] Alexis de Tocqueville, *Democracy in America* (New York: Vintage Books, 1990), vol. I, p. 7.

[9] Vittorio Bufacchi, "Sceptical Democracy," *Political Theory*, 21, 2002, p. 23.

democracy's inherent wild instincts. I think that this is what Socrates as opposed to Plato recognized in his criticism of Athenian democracy and it is what I think Tocqueville means by democracy's wild instincts.

I want to sketch one of the manifestations of democracy's wild instincts that most vexes us today: the tension within democracy between consensus and difference. I want to use this tension as a way of illustrating a dynamic inherent to democratic culture and as a basis for claiming that doubt is essential to democracy in another important sense. I will begin with a familiar view of democratic participation and citizenship.

At the level of theory, the core idea of democracy is the political equality of individuals engaged in the process of governing themselves. Voting is both the symbolic representation and the process through which democracy is realized, according to this familiar view. The vote serves to decontextualize differences among citizens and they become numerical and political equals: one person one vote. In the preface to his brief, but very rich, study of the intellectual origins of liberalism, Pierre Manent asks: "What is an election with universal suffrage, if not that moment when each person strips himself of his social or natural characteristics income, profession, even sex to become a 'simple individual'?"[10] When this notion of the simple individual is grafted onto a vision of the classical notion of the ideal citizen committed to the public good, it suggests a model of the citizens stripped of the contingencies of race or class or religion and so on and an ideal of society is numerical equality.[11] This is one way of expressing the liberal ideal.

There are at least two connected challenges to this liberal ideal. One grows out of the claim that some differences are politically significant differences of gender, race, and sexual orientation, for example. The other grows out of the concrete recognition that democratization as a process is at least in part a matter of *who* constitutes the *demos* and how it is constituted. Consider the second of these challenges first.

The legitimacy of democratic decision making depends on the political process being equally open to all citizens, or at least to legitimate representatives of all citizens. But who are the citizens? Who makes up

[10] Pierre Manent, *An Intellectual History of Liberalism* (Princeton, Princeton University Press, 1994), p. xvi.
[11] See Judith N. Shaklar, *American Citizenship: A Quest for Inclusion* (Cambridge, MA: Harvard University Press, 1991).

the democratic "we" in "We, the People"? The democratic "we" is not found by discovering what citizens have in common by virtue of which they are members of "we." The democratic "we" is made through the political process. Who makes it and how?

Alan Keenan has used this question to illustrate a paradox at the heart of democratic open-endedness. Democratic participation requires openness and inclusion. Yet it cannot be completely open because democratic self-rule is always at a point in time. It is the people of today who rule and for democratic decisions to be made today, what constitutes the people must have sufficient identity and closure for decision and action.[12] Similarly, Charles Taylor has observed that "[d]emocracy is inclusive because it is the government of all the people; but paradoxically, this is also the reason that democracy tends toward exclusion. Exclusion is a by-product of the need, in self-governing societies, of a high degree of cohesion. Democratic states need something like a common identity."[13] It follows from this that constituting democratic citizenship is always imperfect and incomplete. Keenan puts it this way: "[T]he political community is never fully achieved *as* 'a people' as a general and open entity it is instead constantly in formation, continually in the process of calling itself, and being called, into being."[14]

For most of democracy's career, the "we" has been an exclusive club. However, late-twentieth-century democracy has shown an encouraging capacity to expand the membership. The liberal ideal of justice as a race- and gender-blind society has been a powerful force against discrimination and exclusion, enlarging the democratic "we." But herein is the first challenge mentioned in the preceding text. At what price inclusion? It has seemed that inclusion is bought at the expense of politically significant differences. But some would claim that this is an unjustifiable price to pay. What has come to be called *identity politics*, the politics of race, gender, and sexuality that has characterized much of the political terrain of the last few decades, has not simply been a demand for greater inclusion, for opening up the democratic "we." It has challenged liberal assumptions about whether difference matters politically in democratic culture. The liberal notion of democratic

---

[12] Alan Keenan, *Democracy in Question: Democratic Openness in a Time of Political Closure* (Palo Alto, CA: Stanford University Press, 2002), pp. 9–15.

[13] Charles Taylor, "The Dynamics of Democratic Exclusion," *Journal of Democracy*, 9, 1998, p. 143.

[14] *Democracy in Question*, p. 11.

inclusion tends to bleach out difference, albeit for commendable reasons. But it seems that some differences matter politically and cannot be translated without loss into a numerical identity. Being the descendants of slaves in America matters to the self-understanding of African Americans and it is argued, therefore, that it matters for how they see themselves in the political process. To lose that is to lose something essential for achieving democracy's promise. A similar argument has been made by feminists and more recently by gay activists. From the point of view of identity politics, the requirements of inclusion serve to level out differences that matter politically and, in Michel Foucault's sense, to normalize resistant and contrary perspectives to those of the dominant culture.

However, to resist normalization by asserting the political importance of difference is to invite exclusion from the democratic "we" and thus from the processes through which consensus about collective interests are formed. This silences difference in a different way, but it silences it nonetheless.

This claim about difference is highly controversial and hotly debated. The debate illustrates the contested nature of the democratic "we" and the imperfect and incomplete nature of democratic participation. Cohesion and democratic consensus are not made legitimate because they conform to or articulate a common identity. They make whatever identity undergirds democratic decision making at a period in time and by doing so inevitably include the dynamics of inclusion and exclusion. Because the normalizing tendencies of inclusion and the exclusionary tendencies of cohesion and consensus are part of the dynamic of the democratic process, the possibility of resisting and challenging how the democratic "we" is constituted will be a permanent aspect to the democratizing process.

This comes to more than simply acknowledging that dissent has a legitimate place in democratic culture. Cass Sunstein has recently argued, on the basis of psychological experiments and sociological studies, that dissent is not merely legitimate, it is essential because of the conformist tendencies of people in groups.[15] John Dryzek has reached a similar conclusion, based on different reasoning, reasons more similar to Taylor's but with consequences more like Sunstein's.

---

[15] Cass R. Sunstein, *Why Societies Need Dissent* (Cambridge, MA: Harvard University Press, 2003).

Dryzek distinguishes the dynamics of exclusion at the level of political decision making from those in civil society more generally. According to Dryzek, because of the strong tendencies toward exclusion at the level of political decision making and the state, a healthy democracy requires a more oppositional and insurgent civil society as an ongoing challenge to those tendencies. Dryzek summarizes his conclusion this way:

Democratization is largely (though not exclusively) a matter of the progressive recognition and inclusion of different groups in the political life of society. This general inclusion is in turn sometimes manifested in inclusion in the life of the state. However, recognizing that pressures and movements for democratization almost always originate in insurgency in civil society rather than the state, a flourishing oppositional civil society is key to further democratization.[16]

Dissent and insurgency are more than merely disagreement with and opposition to the powers that be. They are born of distrust of the powers that be, even the powers of the democratic consensus, because of the conformist and exclusionary dynamics inherent in them.

There are other such dynamics at the heart of democratic culture, of course. Democratic self-governance requires both individual liberty and the equality of citizens to participate in the offices and opportunities democracy affords. But liberty and equality pull against one another in the ongoing struggle to maximize the scope of individual freedom while seeking to create conditions that overcome the inequalities of ability, class, race, and wealth. Expanded equality must be bought at the expense of individual liberty and vice versa. This tension has organized political theory and political life from the very beginning of modern democracy. I will be considering three other tensions within democratic culture in Chapters 3, 4 and 5: tensions between the claims of public and private life, political conviction and doubt, and individual and common interests. The general point to be made now is that democracy's wild instincts require vigilance and wariness to prevent the tensions inherent in democratic culture from collapsing in one direction or the other. Distrust and dissent in democratic culture are how I characterize this wariness.

---

[16] John S. Dryzek, *Deliberative Democracy and Beyond: Liberals, Critics, Contestations* (Oxford: Oxford University Press, 2000), pp. 113–14.

There is a third form of doubt that I think is essential to democracy. It grows out of the ever-present tendency in democratic culture of one pole of its wild instincts tending to overwhelm the other. To set the stage for this third form, it will be helpful to consider the nature of democratic decision making and the demands different ways of thinking about that process make on democratic citizenship.

The way of formulating the democratic process that has dominated theorizing about democracy for most of its modern history is the liberal model. From Thomas Hobbes through John Rawls, liberalism assumes that the state is a voluntary arrangement in which independent, autonomous, free individuals agree together to exchange certain of their liberties for the advantages individuals receive in return from social arrangements and government. Implied in this conception is that individuals come to the agreement with antecedently formed interests and that the purpose in joining with others is motivated by the desire to maximize those interests through collective decisions, actions, and institutions. When the democratic process is articulated in liberal terms, one gets the view that what is central to democracy is the process of representing and voting one's interests. The vote expresses both individual rights and political equality. Each citizen has the equal right to participate in the democratic process and voting is both the symbolic and concrete expression of that right. Whether one conceives of democracy as direct or representative, the democratic decision-making process is a matter of expressing, brokering, and aggregating the interests of individual citizens. To assure a fair outcome of the decision-making process, liberal democracy requires a neutral framework of procedure and substantive protections of individuals against abuses of power by others, by government, or by the majority.

This, of course, is a highly stylized view of liberal democracy. Liberal theorists are much more varied and nuanced than this.[17] But it is not an unreasonable way of capturing the essential aspects of liberalism. Liberal democracy comes down to voting, the rule of law, and individual rights.

---

[17] See David Held, *Models of Democracy* (Palo Alto, CA: Stanford University Press, 1987) for an excellent treatment of democratic models in general and variations on the liberal model.

In Chapter 1 I considered how at least some social and political theorists have traced democracy's discontent, cynicism, disillusionment, alienation, and disengagement to this liberal conception. It has underwritten a culture of excessive individualism, the argument goes. It has undermined a robust sense of community and common goods. It has reduced citizenship to the periodic ritual of voting. It has turned politics into a blood sport. It has resulted in public policy being formulated by oil companies and pharmaceutical manufacturers.

How might democratic culture and democratic processes be reconceived and reinvigorated in light of its current condition? One of the most interesting and promising proposals has come to be referred to as deliberative democracy. Deliberative theorists share certain of the republic or communitarian criticisms of liberalism, but their inspiration is drawn more from the critical social theory of the German philosopher, Jurgen Habermas, and his theory of communicative action.[18] Habermas has been critical of aspects of both the liberal and the republican or communitarian conceptions of democracy. According to Habermas, both views shift the focus away from what is most important to democracy, the process of consensus formation. Liberals assume that individuals come to the consensus formation process with already formed and clearly articulated interests. Communitarians criticize this atomistic conception of individuals and argue that individuals' interests are constituted by antecedently established common values and that civic life and democratic decision making should operate within that the moral-political consensus of the tradition already shared by citizens. However, for Habermas and other deliberative democrats, liberals underestimate the role the deliberative process can and should play in shaping individual interests. The communitarians overestimate the degree to which citizens in a pluralistic culture antecedently share a sense of civic virtue and the common good. A deliberative model of democracy shifts the center of gravity away from voting, which is the core of citizenship for liberals,[19] and also away from

---

[18] See especially, Jurgen Habermas, *Between Facts and Norms: Contributions to a Discourse Theory of Democracy* (Cambridge, MA: MIT Press, 1996) and "Three Models of Democracy, in *Democracy and Difference: Contesting the Boundaries*, Seyla Benhabib, ed. (Princeton: Princeton University Press, 1996), pp. 21–30.

[19] See, for example, Judith N. Shaklar, *American Citizenship: The Quest for Inclusion* (Cambridge, MA: Harvard University Press, 1991).

civic virtue, which is the core for communitarians.[20] It focuses instead on the deliberative process and on what authentic deliberation should be in democratic culture.

Habermas also criticizes both the liberal and communitarian or republican conceptions because they tend to think about the democratic process primarily in terms of electoral politics and the legislative process. However, at least one of the reasons for democracy's discontent must be this relatively constrained view about where we might make a difference politically and the difficulty we have in seeing how our vote might matter in the effort to bring about genuine change. For deliberative democrats, revitalization of democracy depends, in an important way, on fostering a much broader and more variegated conception of public life and opportunities for citizen participation than electoral politics and the state, a conception of public life that would include nongovernmental organizations (NGOs), civic associations, schools, and even the workplace. I will return to this aspect of the deliberative model in the Chapter 3 where I will place it in the larger context of the contest over the place of public and private life in democratic culture. What I am interested in now are the implications of the deliberative model for the nature of democratic citizenship.

Though the deliberative model grows out of a criticism of liberalism, it inherits from the liberal tradition the recognition that a plurality of conceptions of the good life and values are a given in today's democratic culture. This is not an embrace of moral relativism, at least in the sense that any values are as good as any others. Rather, it is recognition that under conditions of uncertainty, reasonable people can have reasoned disagreement about fundamental values or can give reasonably different weights to shared values. It assumes, therefore, the persistence of moral disagreement in democratic politics. This does not mean that moral disagreements are irresolvable. Rather, it is the recognition that issues become political precisely because, at a given moment in time, there is disagreement at some fundamental level. Amy Gutmann and Dennis Thomas put the point this way:

We do not know whether, if we enjoyed perfect understanding, we would discover uniquely correct resolutions to problems of incompatible values, such

[20] See Sandel, *Democracy's Discontent.*

as those that divide us. . . . But we should be able to recognize that all of us lack that kind of understanding at present. Even if everyone were completely benevolent, some would reasonably give different weight to the many complex factors, moral and empirical, that affect the choice of public policies. Recognizing this human limitation does not imply moral skepticism. It is fully compatible with the belief that there are moral truths, although it does not presuppose this belief. It simply expresses recognition that at any particular moment in history we cannot collectively resolve some moral dilemmas on their own terms. Some dilemmas may have uniquely correct solution, and some may not. But at any historical moment our imperfect understanding, manifest in the fundamental disagreements among the most thoughtful and good-willed citizens, prevents us from definitively distinguishing those that do from those that do not. We live in a state of moral conflict over many issues about which we do not (yet) know the right answer.[21]

Given this point-in-time sense of the persistence of moral disagreement in a pluralistic democracy, democratic deliberation is conditioned by the need for citizens to work together for consensus across disagreement. It is the nature of policy making that even if we can't agree, we must decide. That is what distinguishes politics from ethics textbooks. And we must find ways of deciding that are democratically legitimate despite disagreement.

That we must decide cannot presuppose that at the end of deliberation, the truth will be found and disagreement will disappear. Reasoned disagreement is as much a part of democratic deliberation as agreement. Jean Elshtain has made this aspect of pluralistic democracy the center of her provocative book, *Democracy on Trial*. She begins the book with the ironic observation of John Courtney Murray that "disagreement is a very difficult thing to reach"[22] and she argues that it is the task of a democratic disposition and of democratic institutions to be able to reach disagreement.

What does deliberation within the context of reasoned disagreement require of participants in the democratic process? What does it require of democratic citizenship? One implication is that deliberating democratically requires that citizens recognize that differences among individuals can be *reasoned* differences, even at the level of

---

[21] Amy Gutmann and Dennis Thompson, *Democracy and Disagreement* (Cambridge, MA: Harvard University Press, 1996), p. 25.

[22] Jean Bethke Elshtain, *Democracy on Trial* (Basic Books: New York, 1995), p. xi.

fundamental moral differences, and that this recognition must be reciprocal. This captures at least part of the important place respect for individuals has for liberal democrats. But it also assumes openness to the possibility that my interests, beliefs, and values might change as a result of deliberating with other citizens. This links doubt and democratic deliberation in a third way. Democratic deliberation requires a capacity for self-doubt.

Respect for others implies that as a participant in democratic deliberation and decision making, I accept that individuals whose views and values are different, and even opposed to mine at some fundamental level, might have good and compelling reasons for them, and that deliberation may show that they are even better reasons than my own. That is, to deliberate in good faith is to be prepared both to accept the persistence of moral disagreement as a permanent possibility of the political, and to accept that the deliberative process has an important role in changing and shaping the values of those who participate in deliberation. What this means for my relationship to my own beliefs and values is that I must accept their fallibility and revisibility.

In one sense, recognizing the fallibility of one's beliefs seems obvious and simple. But in another sense, it is highly paradoxical. In those areas of fundamental moral disagreement, for example, the rights of fetuses or of women to choose, aren't these the sorts of issues about which a morally responsible person should have firm conviction, especially in the context of making policy decisions that will bind us all? Can I have conviction about my beliefs and values, the strength of conviction that seems required to act resolutely, and also engage seriously in the process of collective decision making by subjecting them to doubt through the deliberative process? How can doubt of this sort avoid devolving into indifference? But also, how can conviction avoid becoming dogmatic in the face of conflicting views? Dogmatism and indifference are dangers inherent in the dynamics of democratic culture and they are avoidable only if one can have both doubt and conviction in the deliberative process.

At one level this seems relatively easy. Don't negotiation and compromise amount to this? But the challenges of democratic culture, especially of pluralistic culture, run much deeper. Consider, again, the debate over abortion. Should we really expect that at the end of the day, one or the other side in the debate will be found to be wrong? Can public policy decisions await the end of the day? Even if we reached disagreement at so basic a level, public policy must be decided. For this issue, suspending a policy decision is a decision to accept one view rather than another in the debate. Can I believe, and believe deeply at a very basic level, that fetuses have a right to life or that a woman has an inviolate right to decisions about her own reproductive possibilities and still, in good faith and seriously, believe that the disagreement about life and choice is a reasoned disagreement? Doesn't that leave moral conviction a wispy, thin sort of thing?

Yet for a deliberative model of democracy, this is exactly our dilemma. Conviction about things that matter deeply and the capacity for self-doubt at the deepest level about those convictions are both requirements of democratic citizenship.

So far I have argued that doubt is joined to democracy in three ways: as the epistemological field of democracy, wariness and vigilance in the face of democracy's extreme tendencies, and a deep kind of self-doubt. It is necessary to become more systematic about doubt and to sketch what I will call, following Oakeshott, a *politics of skepticism*. I must outline what a politics of skepticism is not. A helpful way to do that is to contrast it with a different version of a skepticism and politics developed by Aryeh Botwinick. Botwinick has argued for skepticism as a way of grounding a view about democratic participation and while I admire his main insight, I depart from the conclusion he draws from it. Saying why will help in articulating the kind of doubt I think is essential to democratic citizenship in the style of the politics of skepticism.

Botwinick's insight is that epistemological assumptions have political consequences. Plato's theory of knowledge and his doubts about the capabilities of the masses to acquire knowledge led to his elitist theory of state, for example, a state ruled by those few who are the true lovers of wisdom. Botwinick's thesis is that radical skepticism, by contrast, favors a politics of broad political participation.

The political implications that I seek to draw from skepticism lie in the direction of a radical egalitarianism. If skepticism in some of its different guises states that none of us is in a position to affirm the rational superiority of his views or values over those of his fellows, then the appropriate political response is to have as many members of society as possible participate in the numerous collective decisions affecting our lives. Skepticism delegitimizes the formation of any permanent hierarchies in society and provides a continually renewing impetus for expansion of political participation.[23]

I am very sympathetic to this insight. But Botwinick thinks the challenge posed by this insight is the need to develop a consistent radically skeptical position, a skeptical position that is not self-referentially defeating in its formulation. This, of course, has been the central issue for epistemologists' in their treatment of skepticism for centuries and the history of philosophy is littered with failed attempts.

In spite of the difficulties of defending a non-self-defeating, radical skepticism, Botwinick also believes that a more mitigated form of skepticism is not up to the task of a skeptical politics either. And he does not think it is enough to settle for a skeptical outlook that is enacted rather than argued for. It is not enough to afford "people an equal opportunity to participate in decisions that shape their lives, without having to shoulder the burden of stating skepticism" (SPP, 9). According to Botwinick, a merely enacted skepticism is not only an easy way out of the hard task for defending skepticism, but this way of thinking about the consequences of skepticism is as consistent with withdrawal as with political participation. Skepticism as merely a way of behaving cannot provide a guarantee for political participation.

The importance of his initial insight notwithstanding, it seems to me that Botwinick asks the wrong sorts of questions of a politics of skepticism. "Can one provide a secure, objectivist foundation for the doctrine of equality and its institutional translation as participation?" (SPP, 25). The assumption behind this question is that participatory democracy requires a philosophical guarantee if it is to fend off the possibilities of either elitist politics or withdrawal from political participation. While his answer is that no objectivist foundation can be given, he nevertheless seeks to move beyond a merely pragmatic defense of political participation by "defending a pragmatic position that gestures toward objectivism by presupposing the philosophical validity of realism to nominalism" (SPP, 25).

My disagreement with Botwinick's version of the politics of skepticism is twofold. First, I think the last thing democracy needs is to be grounded in skepticism or any other view. This is part of the lesson

[23] Aryeh Botwinick, *Skepticism and Political Participation* (Philadelphia: Temple University Press, 1990), p. 7.

learned from critics of John Rawls's attempt to provide a metaphysical foundation for justices as fairness in *A Theory of Justice* and Rawls's subsequent pragmatic reformulation of his view.[24] I will take this issue up in Chapter 4. Second, I think that there simply can be no guarantee that doubt and distrust will lead to participation rather than cynical withdrawal from the political arena. Politics is not the place of guarantees. Enacting skepticism is the best that can be offered and it is enough. My strategy in the Chapters 3 through 5 is to offer historical enactments of the politics of skepticism and to commend them as possibilities for dealing with central issues in contemporary culture. That is, I intend to show its productive possibilities through skepticism's enactment. The politics of skepticism is more than the act of questioning or distrusting political authority. Doubt not only can lead to cynicism, it can also be as trivial and inconsequential as anything else. What the historical case studies in the next chapters will suggest are forms of doubt that have a philosophical depth that is essential for achieving their positive purposes. Socrates is the paradigm for the kind of doubt I have in mind, and for democratic citizenship in the style of the politics of skepticism. In the remainder of this and in Chapter 3, I will examine the nature of his doubt.

I cannot claim Socrates as the paradigm for a politics of skepticism and democratic citizenship without some work because many would argue that Socrates was neither a skeptic nor a democrat. The scholarly literature surrounding Socrates is replete with arguments against each, but I will use Benjamin Barber's formulation because he connects one claim to the other based on a view about democracy that is very much in line with the view I sketched previously. I have cited with approval Barber's claim that democracy begins where certainty ends. Here is how he puts it in connection with Socrates:

Where there is truth or certain knowledge there need be no politics, even though (as Plato warns) politicians and citizens may wantonly ignore truth and

---

[24] See John Rawls, *A Theory of Justice* (Cambridge, MA: Harvard University Press, 1971) and "Justice as Fairness: Political Not Metaphysical," *Philosophy and Public Affairs*, 14, 1985, pp. 223–51; Richard Rorty, "The Priority of Democracy to Philosophy," *Philosophical Papers Vol. 1* (Cambridge: Cambridge University Press, 1991), pp. 175–96; and Amy Gutmann, "Democracy, Philosophy, and Justification," in *Democracy and Difference*, Seyla Benhabib, ed. (Princeton: Princeton University Press, 1996), pp. 340–7.

certain knowledge in pursuit of base interests or raw power. But democratic politics begins where certainty ends. The political question always takes a form something like: 'What shall we do when something has to be done that affects us all? We wish to be reasonable, yet we disagree on means and ends and are without independent ground for making the choice.' For Socrates the point is to secure the independent ground whether through dialectical discourse or pure speculative reasoning. Neither leaves room for politics.[25]

On Barber's view, Socrates can't be a democrat because he denies the conditions of uncertainty that necessitate democratic deliberation.

Obviously the issue of whether Socrates was a skeptic and a democrat is complicated by the fact that our knowledge of the historical Socrates rests primarily on Plato's portrait of him in his earlier dialogues, and to a lesser extent on the dialogues of Xenophon and Aristophanes's play, "The Clouds." Any view about what Socrates believed is speculative at best, depending on the interpretive challenge of disentangling what it is reasonable to attribute to the historical Socrates and what is primarily a creation of Plato and others. We can be fairly confident that Plato was neither a skeptic nor a democrat. But what about Socrates?

It is worth noting that views about whether Socrates was a democrat or not have changed over time. Melissa Lane reminds us that the position various interpreters have taken has had a good deal to do with their attitude about democracy.[26] If one is not a fan of democracy, it is easy to conclude that Socrates was antidemocratic and legitimately so. If one is a friend of democracy, then it is easy to conclude that Socrates must have been antidemocratic, especially because his student, Plato, clearly was. But if one is both a friend of democracy and of Socrates, the task is harder. How do we reconcile Socrates and democracy?

There have been three basic answers to this question. First, there are those who would agree with the antidemocratic characterization of Socrates, but would still criticize Athens for its failure to appreciate democracy's capacity to withstand the kind of dissent Socrates displayed, and perhaps its failure even to recognize its usefulness. This is the view I. F. Stone popularized in *The Trial of Socrates.*[27] This is the

---

[25] "Theory and Practice: Democracy and the Philosopher," p. 45.
[26] Melissa Lane, "Was Socrates a Democrat?" *History Today*, 2002, pp. 42–7.
[27] I. F. Stone, *The Trial of Socrates* (Boston: Little Brown and Co., 1988).

more common attempt to reconcile Socrates and democracy. Second, there are some who have interpreted Plato's earliest dialogues, which most closely approximate Socrates's views rather than his, as an attempt to rehabilitate his teacher's reputation after his trial and death. Plato shows in these early dialogues how Socrates not only declares his allegiance to the Athenian constitution but also never criticizes the central aspects of Athenian democracy. Gregory Vlastos offers the most sophisticated version of this approach, though without claims about Plato's public relations motivations.[28] There is a third view that, while less popular, is gaining currency. According to this view, Socrates, by criticizing Athenian democracy, is enacting a new form of democratic citizenship. This is Dana Villa's view in *Socratic Citizenship*.[29] While this view is consistent with the second view, it makes Socrates out to be more intentionally democratic than Vlastos's interpretation. He doesn't merely approve of the Athenian form of government; he exemplifies what democratic citizenship ought to be. I will offer a version of this view in the Chapter 3.

Whether Socrates was a skeptic is as controversial as whether he was a democrat. We know from Plato's early dialogues that Socrates frequently professed ignorance. The explanation Socrates gave of this in the *Apology* is well-known. Chaerephon, it will be remembered, had gone to Delphi to visit the Oracle there and he asked the Oracle whether anyone was wiser than Socrates. When Chaerephon reported to Socrates that the Oracle had said none was wiser than he, Socrates said he could not believe his ears. After thinking for some time about what the Oracle could have meant he set out to determine the truth of it by seeking those who had a reputation for wisdom. His goal was to show that they were wiser than he was. But as Socrates examined each one he discovered that they only appeared to be wise. Each time "I reflected as I walked away, Well, I am certainly wiser than this man. It is only too likely that neither of us has any knowledge to boast of, but he thinks he knows something which he does not know, whereas I am quite conscious of my ignorance. At any rate it seems that I am wiser than he is to this small extent, that I do not think that I know

[28] Gregory Vlastos, "The Historical Socrates and Athenian Democracy," *Political Theory*, 11, 1983, pp. 495–518.
[29] Dana Villa, *Socratic Citizenship* (Princeton: Princeton University Press, 2001).

what I do not know."[30] This is all familiar. But it is controversial as to how much to make out of it.

Socrates's profession of ignorance is usually read through the eyes of Plato. As such, it is taken either ironically or as the first stage of a method of inquiry that, carried to completion, would result in true knowledge. Barber's position, quoted in the preceding text, assumes this view. Socrates, on this interpretation, is a genuine seeker after truth, and for this reason, Barber argues, he leaves no room for democratic politics.

It has become somewhat more common recently, however, to think of Socrates's profession of ignorance as genuine and to position Socrates within the skeptical tradition that also characterizes later members of Plato's Academy, if not Plato, and that extends to the skeptical way of life exemplified by Pyrrho. This interpretation is largely a result of two trends in recent scholarship. The first, represented by Gregory Vlastos's book, *Socrates: Ironist and Moral Philosopher*, is to take the problem of the historical Socrates seriously by trying to disentangling Socratic views from Plato's Socrates. While Vlastos has offered an exceptional interpretation of the historical Socrates, he does not place much weight on claims that Socrates is a skeptic. The second trend is motivated by attempts to understand how the later skeptical direction of Plato's Academy, under the leadership of Arcesilaus, could have placed Socrates in the developmental line of their brand of skepticism. Christopher Shields has taken up this task. He argues that while Socrates was not a skeptic in Arcesilaus's sense, because Socrates did not employ a generalized procedure for generating "a nearly universal commitment" to suspended judgment in the way Arcesilaus would, nevertheless Arcesilaus might justifiably extend Socratic practice in a way that does not simply misunderstand Socrates.[31] Julia Annis takes the possibility of a skeptical Socrates more seriously even than Shields and also argues that one might even attribute a mild form of skepticism to Plato. These are the features of the Socratic dialogues that Annis thinks support Arcesilaus's interpretation: "Socrates constantly

[30] Plato, "Apology," in *The Complete Dialogues of Plato*, Edith Hamilton and Huntington Cairns, eds. (Princeton: Princeton University Press, 1971), 21 d, pp. 7–8.

[31] Christopher J. Shields, "Socrates among the Skeptics," in *The Socratic Movement*, Paul A. Vander Waerdt, ed. (Ithaca, NY: Cornell University Press, 1994), p. 345.

searches for truth but does not claim to know any; he has strongly held views but does not assert these as reasoned, defensible theses; he limits his philosophical activity to arguing against the rash beliefs of others, showing them how their own premises land them into difficulties."[32]

I merely note in passing Annis's recognition that Socrates was skeptical while nevertheless holding strong convictions. Indeed he was prepared to act on his convictions even in the face of his own death. To the very end of his life he was prepared to question the basis for his own convictions as well as those of his friends who attended him at his death. This is worth remembering in light of the view of many contemporary critics of culture who would join fundamental doubts of the sort that Socrates entertained with cynicism or nihilism and indifference. I will return to the theme of doubt and conviction in Chapter 4.

None of these interpretations of Socrates as a skeptic connect his skepticism with the questions about whether he was a democrat. But as I summarized in the preceding text, Barber makes the correction direct albeit with a negative conclusion. I agree with Barber that the issue of skepticism and the issued of democracy are connected even though he draws the wrong conclusion about Socrates. He argues that because Socrates seeks certainty he cannot be a democrat. I believe, however, that it is the other way around. Because he is a democrat, he must also be skeptical. But skeptical in what sense?

Socrates's skepticism was not based on a general claim about the possibility of certainty. Rather, it was the way he conducted himself in relation to the views of others and ultimately his way of living. His skepticism was enacted rather than argued for. And in this enacted skepticism I think the true heir of the Socratic way of living was Pyrrho of Ellis. Pyrrho was a rough contemporary of Aristotle and a figure even more shadowy than Socrates. My claim to connect Socrates and Pyrrho is not merely an antiquarian interest. We so typically think of skepticism as a technical, epistemological claim, that we forget that it originated in doubts of a moral sort, about whether the pursuit of knowledge was a desirable way to life. This was the force of Pyrrhonian skepticism, beginning with antidotal accounts of Pyrrho, and continuing with the careful formulation of Pyrrhonian skepticism by Sextus Empiricus in

---

[32] Julie Annis, "Plato the Skeptic," in *The Socratic Movement*, Paul A. Vander Waerdt, ed. (Ithaca, NY: Cornell University Press, 1994), p. 332.

the early years of the Christian era. And it was skepticism as a way of life that was to influence Montaigne and, despite his protestations to the contrary, that characterizes David Hume's philosophy of common life. I have argued elsewhere that this Pyrrhonian style of skepticism casts light on how we might interpret contemporary issues about the nature of philosophy in the work of someone such as Richard Rorty, and also about the politics of Michel Foucault.[33] What I will be arguing in this and later chapters is that it characterizes the kind of doubt that is necessary for democratic citizenship. So it is important to say something more about the nature of Pyrrho's skeptical way of living.

The problem of the historical Pyrrho is considerably more difficult than the problem of the historical Socrates. Our knowledge of him is entirely anecdotal and far removed from his own time. In his *Lives of Eminent Philosophers*, Diogenes Laertius reported that "Pyrrho held that there is nothing really existent. . . . [C]ustom and convention govern human action; for no single thing is in itself any more this than that. He led a life consistent with this doctrine, going out of his way for nothing, taking no precautions, but facing all risks as they came."[34] We know, also from Diogenes Laertius, that he traveled to India with Anaxarchus and Alexander's army, and it is suggested that perhaps his contacts in India were the source of his skeptical outlook.[35] Following the example of Pyrrho, his followers were to develop his way of living into a series of strategies for achieving a tranquil life lived in accord with the appearance of things, tradition, and customary laws.

Unlike the epistemological skepticism that followed from Descartes and the negative aspects of Hume – a form of skepticism that cast doubt on the possibility and the reliability of our beliefs generally – the Pyrrhonian skeptics merely cast doubt on *philosophical* beliefs and they did so to live undogmatically. For Pyrrhonism, philosophical theory constituted an attempt to transcend the contingencies of ordinary life by seeking to discover the truth that lay beyond the appearance of things. It was the philosophical attempt to transcend appearances that was the target of the Pyrrhonian strategies. They opposed the

[33] See my *Philosophy in Question: Essays on a Pyrrhonian Theme* (Chicago: The University of Chicago Press, 1988).

[34] Diogenes Laertius, *Lives of Eminent Philosophers*, R. D. Hicks, trans. (Cambridge, MA: Harvard University Press, 1950), vol. II, p. 475.

[35] See Everard Flintoff, "Pyrrho and India," *Phronesis* 25, 1980, pp. 88–108.

philosophers – or *dogmatists*, as they called them – not because they had epistemological qualms about the possibility of knowledge, but because the attempt to transcend the contingent and transitory beliefs and practices of ordinary life would not lead to a happy life.[36]

There were three distinguishable aspects to the Pyrrhonian practice. The first was their strategy of doubt, which, in its general form, opposed any philosophical assertion with an opposite claim of equal strength. The purpose of the strategy was to establish equilibrium between opposing beliefs, rendering a decision between them impossible. The second aspect was the mental state of *epoche* that doubt produced – a state of indifference or suspended judgment about philosophical claims. The third aspect was the feeling of tranquility or quietude that came as a result of the state of indifference. It is this third aspect – *ataraxia* – that was the central point of Pyrrhonism as a way of life. Sextus Empiricus, our best source of knowledge about Pyrrhonism, stressed this early in his *Outlines of Pyrrhonism*: "[T]he Skeptic's end is quietude in respect of matters of opinion and moderate feeling in respect of things unavoidable."[37]

This recipe for mental health against dogmatism had consequences for public conduct as well as private feeling. Skeptics could suspend judgments about reality and truth, but they could not suspend action. Though they accepted no criterion for judging truth, they, nevertheless, had to accept a standard for conducting their lives because they could not withdraw from activity. Again, from Sextus Empiricus:

Adhering . . . to appearances we live in accordance with the normal rules of life, undogmatically, seeing that we cannot remain wholly inactive. And it would seem that this regulation of life is four fold, and one part of it lies in the guidance of Nature, another in the constraint of passions, another in the tradition of laws and customs, and another in the instruction of the arts. . . . But we make all these statements undogmatically (OP, 17).

There are two broad aspects of the politics of skepticism that I wish to draw from these brief accounts of Socrates and the Pyrrhonians. The first is the consistency of doubt and conviction that I noted previously

---

[36] I have treated this in more detail in *Philosophy in Question: Essays on a Pyrrhonian Theme*, ch. 1.

[37] Sextus Empiricus, *Outlines of Pyrrhonism*, R. G. Bury, trans. (Cambridge, MA: Harvard University Press, 1933), p. 19.

and will return to in subsequent chapters. The second has to do with what I called the philosophical depth of their doubt. While the case studies that follow are illustrations of these aspects of the politics of skepticism, I want to discuss what I call the philosophical depth of their skepticism.

The ironic nature of Socratic doubt and the Pyrrhonian strategy of establishing equilibrium between a dogmatist's assertion and its contrary have something important in common. Of course, both are intended to counter dogmatism, ill-founded opinion, or prejudice. They do so not merely by opposing. It is the way their form of doubting intends to establish or heighten the tension between opposing beliefs that will interest me in the case studies in Chapters 3 through 5. Let me offer an illustration from a very different, but perhaps familiar, context.

In the latter part of the twentieth century, Thomas Kuhn's *The Structure of Scientific Revolutions* shattered our traditional way of thinking about science and scientific change. Instead of the view that the growth of science was a matter of rational progression to a true and complete account of reality, he suggested that attention to the history of science shows it to be more like *Gestalt* switches or paradigm shifts, offering up fundamentally different worldviews from one scientific revolution to the next. His view, of course, became the center of intense debate in the philosophy of science for more than two decades. However, in the essay from which Kuhn drew the title of a later book, *The Essential Tension*, he sought to correct the one-sidedness of interpretations of his view. On the usual interpretation, the characteristics most responsible for the development of science are the scientist's ability to overthrow tradition through "divergent thinking," openness, and the capacity to suspend conviction about the most self-evident concepts. But in this later essay Kuhn reports that "both my own experience in scientific research and my reading of the history of science lead me to wonder whether flexibility and open-mindedness have not been too exclusively emphasized as the characteristics of basic science. . . . I must now emphasize that revolutions are but one of two complementary aspects of scientific advance. . . . [O]nly investigations firmly rooted in the scientific tradition are likely to break that tradition and give rise to a new one. That is why I speak of an 'essential tension' implicit in scientific research."[38] Kuhn's insight was that scientific inquiry not only can but must hold onto tradition while revolting against it.

That is suggestive of one way of thinking about the critical stand-point of Socratic and Pyrrhonian doubt. They do not merely oppose and reject traditional or dogmatic opinions. Rather, their skeptical strategies heighten tensions inherent in them to resist dogmatism and to live effectively with the uncertainty and contingency of customary practices. In the next chapters I will argue that this is the way Socrates could be both the deepest critic of Athens and also God's gift, enacting a new paradigm of democratic citizenship, Montaigne could ridicule the beliefs and values of his own culture yet commit himself to them with conviction, and Rousseau could be one of our most compelling champions of individuality and individual freedom, yet argue for the subordination of private interest to the common good. These will be case studies in deep doubt and democracy's essential tensions.

It will not be surprising that deep doubt is concerned with the deepest issues of democratic culture, issues that flow from the tensions and tendencies inherent in democracy. For Socrates it was the tension between the duty of self-examination and self-rule on the one hand, and obedience to Athens on the other. In modern political theory, it is the tension between liberty and equality, for example, or between its dynamics of inclusion and exclusion. More recently we are challenged by issues that flow from the persistence of moral disagreement in a pluralistic culture such as ours, the difficult but inevitable process of refashioning our self-understanding of America before and after Vietnam or September 11, or reconfiguring our place in a transnational context, a context no longer shaped by a balance of powers or the moral clarity of good and evil, a context in which we must find a place for both patriotism and a cosmopolitan outlook. Unfortunately so much of our response to these issues has been formulated in terms of either right wing or left wing, for or against, red state or blue state, patriot or nonpatriot. I want to show in Chapter 3 how the complexity of Socrates's relationship to Athens cannot be captured in claims

[38] Thomas S. Kuhn, *The Essential Tension: Selected Studies in Scientific Tradition and Change* (Chicago: The University of Chicago Press, 1977), pp. 226–7.

that he was either for or against Athenian values. I will suggest how he exemplifies my claim that democracy requires citizens who have both deep convictions and the capacity to subject those convictions to deep doubt. If there were ever a need for this capacity in American culture, it would be now.

3

Private and Public Life

> For Sabina, living in truth, lying neither to ourselves or others, was possible only away from the public; the moment someone keeps an eye on what we do, we involuntarily make allowances for that eye, and nothing we do is truthful. . . . Franz, on the other hand, was certain that the division of life into private and public spheres is the source of all lies: a person is one thing in private and something quite different in public. For Franz, living in truth meant breaking down the barriers between the private and the public.[1]
>
> Milan Kundera, *The Unbearable Lightness of Being*

Socrates was on trial for his life. He appeared before fellow citizens of Athens, defending himself against charges brought by Meletus and others that he had corrupted the youth of Athens and had taught belief in deities other than those of the city. Here is what he said to his jurors as he brought his defense to a close: "Please do not be offended if I tell you the truth. No man on earth who conscientiously opposes either you or any other organized democracy, and flatly prevents a great many wrongs and illegalities from taking place in the state to which he belongs, can possibly escape with his life. The true champion of justice, if he intends to survive even for a short time, must necessarily confine himself to private life and leave politics alone."[2]

---

[1] Milan Kundera, *The Unbearable Lightness of Being* (New York: Harper and Row, 1984), pp. 112–13.

[2] Plato, *Apology* in *Plato: The Collected Works*, Edith Hamilton and Huntington Cairns, eds. (Princeton: Princeton University Press, 1963), p. 17. Subsequent references are to "A" and page number in the text.

The true champion of justice must confine himself to private life and leave politics alone. It is an astonishing claim. Its strangeness, however, would have rung differently in the ears of Socrates's jurors than it does in our own. For his fellow Athenians it is an affront to conventional wisdom. Pericles, Athenian democracy's first citizen, had summed up the conventional view of the matter in his Funeral Oration: "[W]e do not say that a man who takes no interest in politics is a man who minds his own business; we say that he has no business here at all."[3] Participation in the *polis* – the sphere of politics and public life – was both the birth right and the obligation of the Athenian citizen. That was the view of citizenship that Socrates was challenging in his defense.

Participation in public life was not merely the obligation of citizens, however. It was what distinguished those who were free from those who were not. In the conventional Athenian view, it was only within public life that one could be truly free. Today, however, we see freedom and the state in constant tension. But for democratic Athenians, as Aristotle later formulated it, freedom "can only be enjoyed in such a [democratic] state; this they affirm to be the great end of every democracy . . . for all to rule and be ruled in turn."[4] To be mastered by no one but to rule and be ruled in turn – that is, to be free – was only possible through the equal participation of citizens in the *polis*.

Socrates's preference for private life would have been outrageous to Pericles and very probably to his jurors. One could not be a private citizen.

It is common for readers of the *Apology* to recognize that Socrates's response to his accusers is less a defense of himself than an indictment of Athens. From the reader's perspective it is Athens that is on trial.[5] In his trial, Socrates's life – a life devoted to self-examination rather than to the Assembly or politics – was being held up as a challenge to the common Athenian view. Interpreted in the context of what else

---

[3] Thucydides, *History of the Peloponnesian Wars*, Rex Warner, trans. (New York: Penguin Books, 1972), p. 147.

[4] Aristotle, *Politics*, 1317b, *The Basic Works of Aristotle*, Richard McKeon, ed. (New York: Random House, 1966), p. 1265.

[5] For a particularly interesting interpretation of this, see Arlene W. Saxonhouse, *Fear of Diversity: The Birth of Political Science in Greek Thought* (Chicago: University of Chicago Press, 1992), ch. 4. Saxonhouse argues that Socrates blurs the conventional distinction between public and private by taking on the role of father to Athens, chastising Athens as a father would his family.

we know about Socrates, however, the Socratic alternative to Athenian citizenship is not clear cut. We know that Socrates did not necessarily avoid public roles. He had performed his public duty when called upon – he had served in the military, for instance, and he participated in the religious festivals that served a fundamentally public purpose. Though he distrusted politicians and he avoided public offices, he nonetheless believed that conducting himself as he did served the public good of Athens and that it was his civic duty. He said his life was God's gift to Athens. And he was very much a public figure in another sense of the term. The way he lived his life in the seventy or so years before his trial had brought him sufficient public notoriety that Aristophanes's spoof of him in the play, *The Clouds,* could succeed as popular entertainment. His protest to the contrary, he did not shy from public recognition. Yet he claimed in his defense that if one really cared about justice one should live a private life and leave politics alone.

This claim sounds very different to us, however. In a time when distrust of politics and many public institutions is the norm in American life, most of us do not need to be encouraged to leave politics alone. Quite the contrary. Disengagement from the political process and declining participation in public affairs pose the greatest threat to democratic culture. Many political theorists and social observers would argue that it is our preoccupation with private life that causes us to turn our backs to justice and this is the reason for the decline in the quality of politics and public deliberation. Those who worry about the quality of politics and public life these days, worry at least as much about the extent to which so many people have withdrawn from it and retreated to private life, turning inward because of disillusionment with, cynicism about, or alienation from politics. It would seem that we should be asserting the opposite of Socrates's claim today.

The Socratic claim about politics and private life is ambiguous, just as Socrates's life implied an ambivalent attitude about public involvement. The ambiguity is instructive. The ambiguity and his ambivalence are in some ways reflective of our own attitude. Thinking through his claim might provide a useful distance from our own ambivalence to think more clearly about private and public life – about why we worry about the quality of public life at the same time that we are so despairing of it. More than that, however, I will argue that what appears to be Socratic ambivalence represents what I referred to in Chapter 2 as deep doubt, a form of doubt that Socrates embodies. It represents a new paradigm for democratic citizenship. Socratic citizenship offers a richer way of conceiving of public and private life than either that of his jurors or our own. I believe that if we can come to understand his view about citizenship, it might help us rethink our own ambivalence about private life, politics, and the value of public involvement.

What is at stake for us in this issue? Privacy and its relation to public life have become the organizing theme of a good deal of recent political theory, but it is not merely a theoretical issue. Concern about the quality of democratic culture is, in part, a concern about the degree to which so many of us have withdrawn from public involvement, retreating into our private concerns and interests. Where to set the boundary between what is private and what is public is a question implicit in our reactions to the sexual indiscretions of public officials, causing us to ask whether we have a right to know about the personal lives of public figures and how their personal lives affect their public responsibilities. It is what is at stake in our anxiety about the overwhelming capacity of government and social institutions to invade and organize every corner of our lives, an anxiety execrated by the need for greater security in the age of terrorism. But it is also at issue in our dismay over the culture of publicity fostered by "reality" television programs, sexual politics, and confessional journalism. We are cynical about the personal conduct of public officials, confused about the limits of privacy, and confronted with a popular culture that seems pulled between the extremes of public exhibitionism on the one hand, and private narcissism on the other.

The trend toward private narcissism has been a more frequent source of concern expressed by social critics than the emerging culture of publicity – trends that nevertheless exist side by side. Let me give an example of the concern for the trend toward the greater emphasis, in our culture, on a more inward and private life. Richard Sennett has been one of the most influential analysts of the decline of public life. In his book *The Fall of Public Man*, he links the decline directly to this trend. His is a commendable book in many ways, the earliest among a host of studies focused on the declining quality of civic life and its causes. In it he links the decline in public culture to what he calls "the rise of an ideology of intimacy" in contemporary society. Sennett interprets the emergence of the importance of intimacy as our *fleeing* to the private realm, turning the public world into something alien. Here is how he puts it: "[T]he reigning belief today is that closeness between persons is a moral good. The reigning aspiration today is to develop individual personality through experiences of closeness and warmth with others. The reigning myth today is that the evils of society can all be understood as the evils of impersonality, alienation, and coldness."[6] He believes that the resulting characterization of public life in terms of what is impersonal and alien represents a profound cultural shift in our belief about what makes for a meaningful life.

Concern about the self-absorbed tendencies of an individualistic society that has come to prize private pursuits above all else has become a familiar theme of cultural criticism in America. While these analyses are compelling in many ways, trivializing intimacy and conflating private life with individualistic self-absorption does not ring true to much of our concrete experience. While we might agree that the excesses of individualism are dangerous for our culture, it is hard to think that intimacy is its cause. Important aspects of our lives are characterized by the bonds of family, friendships, civic involvement, love, and loyalty that do not fit the narcissistic picture many social critics paint. But these portraits have their effect. The more taken-for-granted the analysis that decries the individualistic direction of private life is, the more difficult it becomes for us to recognize richer forms of intimacy that characterize many of our experiences.

But it is also the case that we find it increasingly difficult to express public values and civic commitments in a language other than that of private interests. That is the point made so compellingly in Robert Bellah et al.'s *Habits of the Heart.* One of the earliest interviews in the book is an all too familiar story of a man driven by career and ambitions for success to the point where his wife divorces him and he become estranged from his children. At a later point in his life he remarries and this time around he throws himself into his family and into community activities. When asked what brought about the change, we would hope for a story of self-discovery, of greater awareness of what was truly important, of coming to realize the importance of family and

---

[6] Richard Sennett, *The Fall of Public Man: On the Social Psychology of Capitalism* (New York: Vantage Books, 1978), p. 259.

civic responsibility for a meaningful life. Instead he replies matter-of-factly that he was into his career then and now he is into his family. The conclusion the authors derive from this and other case studies of middle-class Americans is that the language of individualism and personal preference so dominates our way of making sense of our lives that it has become increasingly difficult to articulate the richness of our social commitments.[7]

We do seem to have lost a capacity for articulating a larger sense of civic commitment and public good and this has motivated any number of social theorists to argue that the only alternative to self-absorption and political indifference is the restoration of an earlier, richer, and thicker sense of public life. The recent controversies in political philosophy between liberalism and communitarianism and between different conceptions of democratic society are cases in point. A range of theorists and critics – from Robert Bellah and his associates to Jurgen Habermas, Michael Sandel, and even Cornel West – have called for a revitalized public sphere.[8] This, of course, is entirely different from what Socrates urges in defending himself before the citizens of Athens. One who really cares about justice should live a private, not a public life.

The theoretical basis for contemporary concern about the declining quality of public or civic culture has typically rested on a critique of classical liberalism and, in particular, the emphasis it places on freedom to pursue one's private interests. So it is with privacy that we must begin if we are to appreciate the significance of the concern about the declining quality of and engagement in public life.

In the eighteenth and nineteenth centuries, the liberal conception of privacy developed out of a deep concern about the intrusive power

---

[7] Robert Bellah et al. *Habits of the Heart: Individualism and Commitment in American Life* (Berkeley: University of California Press, 1985) pp. 20–1.

[8] See, for example: Ralph Ketcham, *Individualism and Public Life: A Modern Dilemma* (Oxford: Basil Blackwell, 1987); Jurgen Habermas, *The Structural Transformation of the Public Sphere* (Cambridge, MA: MIT Press, 1988); Michael Sandel, *Liberalism and the Limits of Justice* (Cambridge: Cambridge University Press, 1982) and *Democracy's Discontent: America in Search of a Public Philosophy* (Cambridge, MA: Harvard University Press, 1996); Robert Bellah, Richard Madsen, William M. Sullivan, Ann Swindler, and Steven M. Tipton, *The Good Society* (New York: Alfred A. Knopf, 1991); Cornel West, *Race Matters* (Boston: Beacon Press, 1993) and his recent *Democracy Matters* (New York: Penguin Books, 2004); and Jean Bethke Elshtain, *Democracy on Trial* (New York: Basic Books, 1995).

of the state, and of society generally, into areas of individual conduct. Such an intrusive state had been supported by a philosophical theory common to Plato and Aristotle and characteristic of political theory into the seventeenth century, a view in which the state was thought to be essential for fostering human nature and the realization of the good life. It was against this older view of the role of the state that John Stuart Mill's *On Liberty*, for example, was directed. Mill observed that "the ancient commonwealths thought themselves entitled to practice, and the ancient philosophers countenanced the regulation of every part of private conduct by public authority, on the ground that the State had a deep interest in the whole bodily and mental discipline of every one of its citizens."[9] Mill allowed that while this may have been an appropriate way of conceptualizing the role of the state in relation to its citizens in a small republic under constant threat by its enemies, it is wholly unacceptable in modern society. Because of the modern state's extraordinary capacity to intrude and control every aspect of the lives of citizens, such an intrusive state is despotic. Against the modern threat of "despotism of society over the individual," Mill was to give the clearest statement of the core principle of liberalism: "The only freedom which deserves the name is that of pursuing our own good in our own way, so long as we do not attempt to deprive others of theirs or impede their efforts to obtain it" (OL, 12). This space of individual freedom constitutes the domain of private life, a domain characterized by noninterference from the state or others. The implication of this liberal conception of privacy is that it is no business of the state how one conducts one's life in private. The important implication of this view, the implication that marks its difference from ancient views of the state, is that the state should remain neutral about how citizens conduct their lives in private – about the many possible ways its citizens chose to live their lives – so long as they conduct their lives in ways that do not interfere with the similar freedom of others. It follows from this that the line between what is private and what is public is sharply drawn, dividing what is purely personal from what is of collective, and therefore, state interest. For classical liberals such as Mill, the public sphere is always held in a certain suspicion because of its overwhelming

9 John Stuart Mill, *On Liberty* (Indianapolis: Hackett Publishing Company, 1978) p. 12. Subsequent references are to "OL" and page number in the text.

tendency to appropriate more and more aspects of individuals' private lives as matters of collective interest, and thus the boundary of private freedom must be clear and strong. As inheritors of this liberal tradition, we typically understand private life, then, in tension with the public world. Private life is the space of the individual, the space we must constantly guard against the threat of public intrusions.

Mill was to mark out the sphere of privacy by negation[10] as the sphere of noninterference and noncoercion. But as we have come to think about privacy more systematically, especially as constitutional law has evolved and articulated a *right* to privacy, this essentially negative characterization has been filled in more substantive ways, tying the right to privacy to both the right of self-presentation or informational privacy – our control over what others and the government can know about us – and personal autonomy – our right to choose for ourselves in intimate and personal matters. This more substantive concept of privacy rights has evolved through a series of Supreme Court decisions having to do first with unauthorized use of personal information in libel cases and then in cases having to do with sexual intimacy and reproduction. This transition was completed in the Supreme Court decision in *Roe v. Wade,* which was based on an interpretation of privacy as the right to make choices in those areas of one's life that are most intimate and central to personal autonomy and dignity.

Both the ideas of informational privacy and the right to autonomous choice are being contested today. The scope of one's right to informational privacy is being tested by the need for greater security in the face of the greater threat of terrorism. The U.S. Patriot Act has become the most politically charged focal point for this debate. It is also being tested because of the greater capacity, with the convergence of computer technology and the Human Genome Project, to collect genetic information, and, as a result, the greater capacity of insurance companies or employers to have access to that information. These have made our historic concerns about informational privacy even more acute.

Oddly, the scope of informational privacy is also being tested in popular culture, but in an opposite way. One only needs to spend a

---

[10] See Isaiah Berlin, "Two Concepts of Rules," in *Four Essays on Liberty* (Oxford: Oxford University Press, 1996), pp. 118–72.

day watching television talk shows, "reality television" programs, and docudramas of crimes, emergency rooms, and disasters to realize the ever-widening boundaries of self-presentation and self-disclosure, and thus, the shrinking private space. A program devoted to mothers who marry their daughters' boyfriends draws a half-dozen pairs of mothers and daughters revealing their most intimate conflicts to an audience of millions. Young men and women agree to live together in a house under constant television surveillance, having their conversations, squabbles, and sexual encounters broadcast in prime time for the entire world to enjoy. *People Magazine* has replaced the confessional and the analyst's couch as the venue for working out the trauma of childhood sexual abuse. Some of this, of course, is healthy as we break out of more Victorian sensibilities, but some is frankly disturbing. We are a culture in which publicity is becoming the norm for ordinary lives swept along as much by exhibitionism in the age of media as by the invasion of private life by the U.S. Patriot Act or by the capacities of information and genetic technologies.

Everything is also becoming political. Feminists have convincingly argued that *public* and *private* are not benign category distinctions. As the introduction to one collection of essays puts it, "the public/private split is a metaphor for the social patterning of gender."[11] Feminists have argued that the sacred status of the private – of male privacy, that is – and with it, the devalued status of domestic life, has aided and abetted the subjugation of women, legal indifference to child and spouse abuse, administration of reproduction, and so on. They have reacted by demanding public attention to domestic, heretofore private issues, turning the family and even women's bodies – so far as health, reproduction, and exploitation are concerned – into politically significant phenomena. "The personal is the political" is the critical mantra of many feminists. This is also the case for many gay activists. In the sexual politics of today, privacy is identified with the closet, hiding what is shameful, or the need in a homophobic culture to conceal one's sexuality orientation.[12] Liberation requires that we break

---

[11] Eva Gamarnikow et al., eds. *The Public and the Private* (London: Heinemann, 1983), p. 5.
[12] See, for example, Richard D. Mohr, *Gay Ideas: Outing and Other Controversies* (Boston: Beacon Press, 1992).

with the constraining idea that sexuality is a private matter to be hidden away.

Ironically, both the liberal defense of private life and feminist and gay critiques of liberal privacy are offered in the name of securing our freedom, but they are played out in completely opposite ways. The one defends personal freedom by securing a sphere of privacy, the other by rejecting that sphere. Unfortunately, however, both strategies risk being self-defeating.

The inner contradiction of liberal individualism and the pursuit of private freedom has been extensively discussed. Psychiatrists, philosophers, and social observers from many different viewpoints have long worried about the self-defeating strategies of individualistic self-fulfillment and the dangers of political indifference in a society too much in love with private life. In the name of greater autonomy, the individualistic strategies to achieve it often result in a greater sense of alienation both personal and political.

Less attention has been paid, however, to the insidious ways in which various politicizing strategies undertaken for the purposes of expanded freedom – particularly by socially marginalized groups – can contribute to the reduction of personal freedom by inviting the further expansion of public power. Michel Foucault's genealogy of modern social institutions and modern power is the most notable exception. His analyses should make us cautious in our drive to expand the boundaries of the political to increase freedom. His studies of the emergence of the asylum and psychiatry, the prison, the medical clinic, and modern notions of sexuality illuminate the variety of ways modern society is capable of reducing freedom by organizing, administering, normalizing, and co-opting individuals.[13] Following Foucault's analysis, I worry that the politics of recognition and the politicization of private life in the name of greater freedom of one sort pay a price in the reduction of freedom of another. The price is that everything becomes a proper object for public intervention and administration, what the classical liberal most feared. Privacy staked its claim against the intrusive capabilities of the state and to reject privacy – albeit

[13] See Michel Foucault, *Madness and Civilization* (New York: Random House, 1965); *The Birth of the Clinic* (London: Tavistock, 1973); *Discipline and Punish* (New York: Random House, 1979); and *The History of Sexuality* (New York: Random House, 1980).

from legitimate concerns – gains with one hand and gives with the other.

Some feminists have worried about this consequence of the critique of liberal privacy as well. Jean Cohen, for example, has argued that the legitimate unmasking by feminists of the gendered domination inherent in the prevailing ways of distinguishing public and private, also obscures the very important role the right to privacy must play in enhancing freedom, equality, and plurality.[14] Jean Elshtain has made a similar point in her book *Public Man, Private Woman*:

> to the extent that the public world, with all its political, economic, bureaucratic force, invades and erodes the private sphere, it, not the private world, should be the target of the social rebel and feminist critic. To promote a politics of displacement that further erodes the terms of the private sphere and all that stands between us and the coarse power or market-ridden definition of all life, is to repress discourse on public political issues even as one simultaneously takes the symptoms of its destructive effects as the "good news" that radical change is just around the corner.[15]

For Elshtain, the target of feminist criticism should be male-dominated social structures, not private life. To politicize private life undercuts an essential domain of freedom that is necessary if we are to resist the already existing tendency toward an all-encompassing government involvement in our lives.

Cohen's and Elshtain's worries are borne out in an attack on the liberal conception of privacy from a quite different position on the political spectrum, an attack aimed at producing a very different result than the feminist critique. From the point of view of some social conservatives, the idea that a woman has a constitutionally protected right to choose in the case of abortion is seen as the *consequence* of the liberal conception of privacy. Abortion is arguably the most polarizing moral debate in recent memory, and it is at base a debate about the scope of privacy. Does abortion fall within the scope of a woman's decisional autonomy or is it an issue of legitimate public interest to protect the

---

[14] Jean L. Cohen, "Democracy, Difference, and the Right of Privacy," in *Democracy and Difference: Contesting the Boundaries of the Political*, Seyla Benhabib, ed. (Princeton: Princeton University Press, 1996), pp. 187–217.

[15] Jean Bethke Elshtain, *Public Man, Private Woman: Women in Social and Political Thought* (Princeton: Princeton University Press, 1981), p. 333.

life of a fetus? As difficult and controversial as the issue of abortion has become, it is an instance of a more general philosophical and constitutional debate about whether there is a constitutional right to privacy in this sense, and if so, whether it extends to decisional autonomy in matters of reproduction, marriage, and same-sex relationships. These have become the battleground in the culture wars that have dominated and polarized American politics in recent decades.

Michael Sandel's analysis will serve as an example of how the liberal conception of privacy organizes the battleground in ways very different from feminist concerns about privacy. Sandel has argued that a construal of privacy as a right to decisional autonomy is part of a larger problem with liberalism. It is worth spending some time with his argument. His interest is both theoretical and concretely political. In his earlier book, *Liberalism and the Limits of Justice*, Sandel argued against the theoretical foundations of liberalism. His target was John Rawls's very influential theory of justice. Against Rawls, Sandel argued that the conception of the individual upon which Rawls's liberalism rests is incoherent and inadequate as a foundation for Rawls's own social vision. I will consider the liberal conception of the individual in Chapter 5. In Sandel's more recent book, *Democracy's Discontent*, Sandel seeks to revive the republic tradition of civic virtue as an alternative to liberalism and its problems. In both cases, the source of Sandel's concern is with the liberal assumption that the democratic state must be neutral among ways of life and competing values, the view that underwrites the liberal conception of privacy and that underwrites the controversial *Roe v. Wade* interpretation of the right to privacy.

Privacy, of course, was not included among the rights guaranteed in the Constitution. It has evolved through a number of Supreme Court decisions, culminating, at least for now, in the interpretation given in *Roe v. Wade*. Sandel's historical argument is that the constitutional interpretation of privacy rights has shifted from support of the right of informational privacy to a very different claim in *Roe v. Wade*, which extends constitutional protection to the right of decisional autonomy. His theoretical argument is that the idea of a right to decisional autonomy is both conceptually flawed and destructive of democracy in practice. As a practical matter, Sandel believes that there are some issues about which the state should not remain neutral. With respect to marriage, for example, he would interpret government interest in marriage not

as government interest in defending the privacy of intimate relationships as such, but rather as a defense of the intimacy of the marriage
relationship as an important social institution. In the case of abortion,
he claims that the supposed neutrality of the law is a position in the
controversy. He argues that the claimed neutrality in *Roe v. Wade* "presupposes a particular answer to the question it purported to bracket"
(DD, 101). Theoretically, he argues that decisional autonomy presupposes the liberal, voluntarist conception of the self: the idea that the
self is antecedent to society and chooses its ends independent of its
social involvements. He takes the right of decisional autonomy to rest
on what he calls the "unencumbered self," the liberal idea that individuals choose their interests antecedent to social involvements. The
unencumbered self, according to Sandel, implies the impossible idea
that we can bracket out the influences of tradition, culture, or our
social situation in deciding our interests. It entails that the particular
ties and attachments of such things as family or religion or community
are irrelevant for matters of public concern. Here is Sandel's summary
of the argument against the right of decisional autonomy:

First, attempts to be neutral among competing conceptions of morality or
religion often rely on implicit answers to the controversies they purport to
bracket, as the abortion example illustrates. Second, treating persons as freely
choosing, independent selves may fail to respect persons encumbered by convictions that do not admit the independences the liberal self-image requires.
In different ways, the Sabbath observers in Connecticut, the victims of racial
defamation in Chicago, the Holocaust survivors in Skokie, the feminists against
pornography in Indianapolis, the homosexuals denied privacy in Georgia, and
the traditional mothers and homemakers impoverished by divorce are all situated selves with good reason to resist the demand to bracket their identities for
the sake of political agreement; their concerns cannot be translated without
loss into the voluntarist, individuated terms on which the procedural republic
insists. (DD, 116)

Sandel's argument is typical of many republican-oriented, communitarian theorists – from both the right and the left on the political
spectrum – who lay the problems of democratic culture at the door of
liberalism. For reasons very different from feminist critics, they argue
against privacy in favor of the view that individuals are "constituted by"
communally held values and that what must be cultivated is public life
that nurtures communal values such as family, religious convictions,

neighborhood, and so on, and that fosters associational and civic engagement. According to republican-minded communitarians, liberalism flattens out important moral and cultural values by relegating them to private, autonomous choices. This, they claim, yields a too thin conception of community and civic life. Again from Sandel:

> [T]he republican tradition emphasizes the need to cultivate citizenship through particular ties and attachments. More than a legal condition, citizenship requires certain habits and dispositions, a concern for the whole, an orientation to the common good. But these qualities cannot be taken as given. They require constant cultivation. Family, neighborhood, religion, trade unions, reform movements, and local government all offer examples of practices that have at times served to educate people in the exercise of citizenship by cultivating the habits of membership and orienting people to common goods beyond private ends. A public life that fails to nurture these practices or is indifferent to their fate fails to cultivate the virtues essential to self-government as the republican tradition conceives it.
>
> But as we have seen, the procedural republic is often inhospitable to claims premised on self-definitions such as these. It brackets the constitutive ties that the republic tradition sees as essential to political education. The thin pluralism the procedural republic provides is not only a problem for its own sake; it also erodes the resources of self-government. (DD, 117)

It is a matter of reasoned disagreement whether liberalism must rest on a conception of the "unencumbered self" as Sandel and others have claimed. I will turn to this disagreement in Chapter 5. And it is also a matter of reasoned disagreement whether liberalism is inhospitable or indifferent to community-oriented values. I will take this issue up in Chapter 4. The point I wish to make now is that the nature of private and public life has become the focal point for rethinking the quality of democratic culture and the nature of democratic citizenship, and it is battleground for such fundamental social issues as abortion, the nature of the family, and gay marriage. So there is a great deal at stake both theoretically and practically in how we think about public and private life.

When we attempt to sort through the cultural phenomena and the philosophical arguments about private and public life, however, we tend to be pulled in contradictory directions. It is difficult not to despair over the impoverishment of public life and civic culture and to believe that the cause is connected with the excesses of individualism.

Yet we also worry about the widening encroachment of the state and society into our private lives. We take it as a mark of social progress that there is greater public policy attention to issues such as domestic violence and that there is a decreasing need to hide one's sexual orientation. Yet we worry about the culture of publicity and the diminishing space of intimacy. There is a deep ambivalence in our thinking and in our practices about the scope, value, and boundaries between private and public life. At least part of the reason for this ambivalence is that *public* and *private* are terms that have been made to work so many venues for so many different purposes. Our confusions about private and public life are caused, in part, by this fact. Private has been distinguished from public for moral, epistemological, legal, political, psychological, and social purposes. These different purposes do not always cut at the same joint. Consider the different ways the terms have figured in the philosophical literature.

At the beginning of the modern age, René Descartes identified the private sphere with the inner, subjective realm of the mind to which the consciousness individual, alone, had access. Privacy, for Descartes, was primarily an epistemological concept, marking off the immediacy of our experience of ourselves as conscious beings from what is mediated to us through our ideas. For John Locke, however, privacy took on an additional political role, first in terms of his argument for private property rights – the legitimacy of ownership of that with which one mixes one's labor – and by extension, to include ownership of one's self and body. Rousseau gave privacy a primarily psychological cast. He identified it with intimacy in relationship to one's self that he called *amour de soi* – a form of self-love and self-dependency that Kant would give an ethical formulation in terms of autonomy. These, of course, do not come to exactly the same thing. Something similar can be said of the concept of the public realm. Today we too frequently identify it with the realm of politics, but historically it has been used to cover the sphere of openness and impartiality, to characterize what is common to all as distinct from personal interest, and, more broadly, to include the associational aspects of civic culture. Again, while these constitute a family of terms, they imply different things. One can find arguments in the philosophical literature for the centrality of each of these different uses of public and private. Added to this is recognition that the distinction between what is public and what is private is not so much a matter of conceptual geography – though it is in part that – as it is the source of political dispute and disagreement, as we have seen in the feminist critiques and Sandel's argument against the *Roe v. Wade* interpretation. To borrow the phrase that William Connolly reintroduced to political theory, public and private are "essentially contested concepts."[16] That is, they are by nature political concepts and as such they will be drawn and redrawn by ongoing disagreement, conflict, and struggle. They are concepts that are contested in and of themselves and contested in relation to one another. How we understand them depends on where we are in the contest.

It is not just that there is disagreement, however. The shape of the disagreement sometimes turns on historical baggage the concepts still carry. As I suggested in the preceding text, that history reveals a mix of both epistemological and political motives. But it is also marked by a fundamental shift from ancient to modern ways of thinking about privacy; from the context in which Socrates defended his life before his Athenian peers to modern formulations. Appreciating that shift and thinking about what Socrates may have meant by living a private, not a public life, may be helpful in thinking through the contested nature of public and private life in contemporary culture and thinking.

Hannah Arendt's influential interpretation in *The Human Condition* of the transformation of the public and private spheres from the Greeks to the modern age will provide a useful starting point. Though her view has been criticized on the basis of more subtle accounts of the Greeks,[17] the general contours of it still provide important insights.

In *The Human Condition*, Arendt identifies the modern age with the emergence of "society." *Society* is her special term to distinguish the modern state from the idea of the Greek *polis* or city-state. The focus of her analysis is on the classical Greek understanding of public and private life and how, according to her analysis, the rise of modern society radically altered the ancient distinction, shifting the location of freedom from the public to the private domain.

[16] William E. Connolly, *The Terms of Political Discourse* (Princeton: Princeton University Press, 1993).

[17] Arlene W. Saxonhouse, "Classical Greek Conceptions of Public and Private," in *Public and Private in Social Life*, S. I. Benn and G. F. Gaus, eds. (London: St. Martins Press, 1983), p. 380–1.

Originally the ancient Greeks had distinguished the *polis* from the household. In Arendt's terms:

> [T]he distinctive trait of the household sphere was that in it men lived together because they were driven by their wants and needs. The driving force was life itself . . . necessity ruled over all activities performed in it. The realm of the *polis*, on the contrary, was the sphere of freedom . . . the *polis* was distinguished from the household in that it knew only 'equals,' whereas the household was the center of the strictest inequality.[18]

To gloss her analysis, the household was concerned with administering the basic necessities of life and thus with labor and work – which Arendt identifies with the merely animal. The life of action, as distinct from labor, was what was distinctive about the human condition qua human as distinct from what is animal about us. And action was only possible within the *polis*. Action referred to associations among equals in their public roles and political relations, where no one was master, no one mastered. Thus action, that is, truly human freedom, would only be realized through participation in the affairs of the *polis*. One can already anticipate how feminists are reacting to these vestiges in our modern concepts of the ancient understanding of the public space of men and the privacy of the household that is hidden and unfree.

Arendt's central claim is that, with the rise of modern society, the Greek understanding of the function of the *polis* as the place of activity among equal citizens gets transformed into a domain of public administration. Society replaces the *polis*. Society is characterized not by discourse, citizenship, and freedom, but by administration or taking over functions of the household. With this transformation, a very different conception of privacy develops. Privacy comes to be contrasted not with a realm of free citizens, but with the administrative functions of the state. Privacy becomes identified with the inmost part of ourselves that remains free of the ever-expanding encroachment of social administration. Social administration requires conformity to manage efficiently the necessities of life. Privacy, by contrast, becomes the place of individuality, the place where individuals are free to conduct their lives in their own ways. Arendt puts it this way: "[S]ociety expects from

---

[18] Hannah Arendt, *The Human Condition* (Chicago: University of Chicago Press, 1958), p. 30.

each of its members a certain kind of behavior, imposing innumerable and various rules, all of which tend to 'normalize' its members, to make them behave to exclude spontaneous action or outstanding achievement."[19] The private realm, by contrast, becomes the shelter for freedom, autonomy, and originality against the social drive for conformity.

Modern political theory reflects this shift from the *polis* to society. From the seventeeth century forward, the legitimate society is usually conceived of as the voluntary arrangement of individuals associating for mutual benefit. This view casts the proper function of society as maximizing the conditions in which individual needs and interests can be met. Rather than a space for freedom, mutuality, and discourse, society constitutes a limit on personal freedom for the purpose of effectively realizing collective interests. The consequences Arendt draws from this transition from the idea of the *polis* to society are familiar. In place of action, freedom, and citizenship in the *polis*, we get politicians, bureaucrats, decision-theorists, technical advisors, experts, public health officials, and social workers. In place of individuality and diversity, we get mass culture. It was Rousseau who most clearly understood the threat of society to individuality. He lamented in the *First Discourse* that society reduces individuality, uniqueness, and genius to the common level of its age. Nietzsche expressed a similar concern. He claimed that modern social institutions produced herd-animalization. And in our own day, Michel Foucault's studies of modern social institutions reveal how modernity brings into being and is reinforced by distinctive forms of normalizing power that aim at achieving efficiency over populations by producing docile individuals.

As I suggested, there has also been an epistemological agenda that undergirds the social and political agenda of modernity. It pulls, however, at a slightly different angle. Our modern notion of privacy links Descartes's epistemology, Locke's political theory, and Rousseau's social psychology. It links Descartes's quest for certainty, which he discovered in the immediacy of private, inner representations, to Locke's theory of individual rights, and also to Rousseau's psychology of self-love and self-dependency in the face of mass culture. This linkage of epistemological and political agendas is not stable, however.

[19] *The Human Condition*, p. 40.

After Descartes, philosophers were to give priority to the publicly accessible and intersubjective realm so far as knowledge was concerned, relegating Cartesian privacy to the merely subjective. Following Locke and Rousseau, however, political and social theory was to give priority to privacy so far as rights, individuality, and freedom were concerned. Moral theory, however, was to pull both ways. To the extent that morality is concerned with authenticity, it gives priority to private autonomy. To the extent that it is concerned with moral deliberation it identifies the private with the partial and prejudicial, giving deliberative priority to impartiality and generality. What complicates the matter even further is that when private life extends beyond the individual to the family, our modern conception retains vestiges of the ancient view of the inferior and hidden status accorded domestic life. This ancient holdover is what feminist critics have brought to the foreground, showing how the combination of the sacred domain of privacy and the devalued status of domestic life define privacy in terms of male privacy and serves to reinforce the control of women as well as public neglect of domestic issues. For now, however, the point I want to draw from this history is that the epistemological dimension of the public realm has entered contemporary debate alongside the political issues of the locus of freedom and the status of domestic life. The consequence of this linkage is a fundamental tension at the core of both concepts. Our concepts of public and private life are as confused as they are contested. It is in the context of this tension that I return to Socrates.

There has been considerable dispute about how to interpret Socrates's attitude about public life and public roles and his supposed preference for private life. Some scholars interpret him as merely reflecting antidemocratic sentiments. Others interpret him as primarily apolitical, drawing a sharp distinction between his project of self-examination and affairs of the *polis*, and they take his rejection of public life in the *Apology* as their evidence. On this interpretation, the skeptical side of Socrates's claim that he lacks moral wisdom is taken as the crucial point. It is claimed that skepticism must inevitably lead to political passivity because a politically active life would imply, contrary to skepticism, that one had moral knowledge. Still other interpreters focus primarily on the prudential aspects of Socrates's claim, arguing that Socrates is simply being realistic about the practical impossibility of establishing a just political order in Athens, recognizing the very real personal risks of opposing those in power.[20]

Let's begin with this last interpretation. Though the initial reason Socrates gave for his claim appeared to be prudential – no man who consciously opposes any organized democracy can hope to escape with his life, is the way he put it – because of other things we know about Socrates we cannot take his remarks about escaping with his life at face value. It is clear from other parts of the *Apology*, as well as from what he concludes in the *Crito* and his discussions of death in the *Phaedo*, that he believed that if one practices philosophy, one should not fear death. Seen in the context of his attitude about death, the prudential interpretation cannot be taken seriously. There must be a deeper rationale for rejecting public roles. Getting at that deeper rationale is not merely an academic interest. I think it will show something important for how we are pulled between conflicting claims about private and public life.

Socrates's central claim is that a private rather than a public life serves the cause of justice. That alone suggests that he is not apolitical and not merely acquiescing in the face of moral skepticism. He was neither urging political quietism nor waiting for the emergence of moral experts to rule the city. He distrusted the public realm of "political appointments, secret societies, and party organizations" and distrusted the opinions of the many that circulate there, and he distrusted them because that is not where justice is to be found. Justice is to be found in private life through care of the soul, not by participating in the Assembly. Furthermore, through care of the soul Socrates believes that we will be better able to negotiate the deceits and uncertainties of public life.

Montaigne – to whom I shall turn more fully in Chapter 4 – appreciated the significance of Socrates's claim that the source of justice is to be found in private life, and his formulation will help clarify, I think, the position Socrates was taking. Montaigne's essay "Of Repentance" was concerned with the ease with which one can adopt a public role compared with the difficulty of ordering one's private life. "It is a rare

---

[20] See, for example, the accounts of I. F. Stone, *The Trial of Socrates* (Boston: Little, Brown and Company, 1988), pt. I; Thomas C. Brickhouse and Nicholas D. Smith, *Socrates on Trial* (Princeton: Princeton University Press, 1989), p. 167ff; and Richard Kraut, *Socrates and the State* (Princeton: Princeton University Press, 1984), ch. IV.

life," Montaigne had written, "that remains well ordered even in private. Any man can play his part in the side show and represent a worthy man on the boards; but to be disciplined within, in his own bosom, where all is permissible, where all is concealed – that is the point."[21] In public we put on masks, adopt social roles, clothe ourselves in the fashions we find there, curry favor from our audience through flattery and dissimulation, and trade in the vanity of words. A well-ordered private life is the only way of negotiating such a world intact. I think this is also the point Socrates was making.

What I wish to focus on now, however, is the nature of private life that Socrates claimed to be the source of justice. It differs fundamentally from the conventional view of his jurors and but it also differs from our own, and it is this difference that is my rationale for bringing him together with our current debates. The initial point to make about Socrates's view is that private life is neither the domain of the household, as his jurors would understand it, nor is it the inner life of the individual, as we have come to understand it, at least since Descartes and Rousseau. Its contrast with our own understanding is easiest to see initially. What Socrates means by private life is precisely the sort of life he had led. His life had been neither withdrawn nor individualistic. It had been an inquiring life lived out in the open and among others. Socrates sought the virtuous life neither in the Assembly – the institutionalized public sphere – nor in the privacy of the household nor in the hermit's hut. He sought it in the *agora*, in the commerce of Athenians, slaves, and aliens, with friend and stranger alike. The life well lived was indeed an inwardly directed life so far as it concerned the condition of the soul, but it was not individualistic in our modern sense. His way of self-examination was through conversation with others about the life worth living. This discursive dimension of Socrates's way of living is not merely Plato's literary device. The Socratic life is *essentially* social. His examination of his own life is *essentially* dialogical. That is, it is not reducible to the solitary reveries of his conversational partners.

Again, Montaigne understood this aspect of Socrates. He also captured this essentially social feature of private life, using as his model the intimacy of friendship which, I think, usefully illuminates the Socratic

[21] Michel de Montaigne, *The Complete Essays of Montaigne*, Donald M. Frame, trans. (Palo Alto, CA: Stanford University Press, 1958), p. 613.

view. Montaigne described friendship as the mingling of souls so complete that it "efface[d] the seam that joined them."[22] In the bland but useful terminology of analytic philosophy it is a "we-intending," intentions that are not decomposable as interests of a separate individual. It is what Charles Taylor – drawing out features of the work of Heidegger, Wittgenstein, and Bakhtin – has in mind when he argues that an essential aspect of our understanding of ourselves in both intimate and public roles is understanding dialogical actions.[23] So when Socrates urges private life as the true source of justices, he does not have an individualistic life in mind.

How Socrates's view of private life differed from his jurors is more complicated, but it is also important for how we might make sense of our own confusions about the claims of public and private life. As a starting point it is useful to remember that Socrates reported in his trial that he was set on this way of living by the Oracle who declared that none was wiser than he. He was guided in his way of living by his god – his inner voice – for whom his way of living was a duty. To cease living the way he did would be disobedience to the god. Here is how he put it to his judges:

> Perhaps someone may say, But surely, Socrates, after you have left us you can spend the rest of your life minding your own business.
>
> This is the hardest thing of all to make some of you understand. If I say that this would be disobedience to God, and that is why I cannot 'mind my own business,' you will not believe that I am serious. If on the other hand I tell you that to let no day pass without discussing goodness and all the other subjects about which you hear me talking and examining both myself and others is really the very best thing that a man can do, an that life without this sort of examination is not worth living, you will be even less inclined to believe me. (A, p. 23)

Living the way he did was fulfilling his duty to the god. But he also claimed he – or more precisely, his way of living – was God's gift to Athens. "If you put me to death, you will not easily find anyone to take my place. It is literally true, even if it sounds rather comical, that

---

[22] *Essays*, p. 139.

[23] Charles Taylor, "The Dialogical Self," in *The Interpretive Turn: Philosophy, Science, Culture*, David R. Hiley, James F. Bohman, and Richard Schusterman, eds. (Ithaca, NY: Cornell University Press, 1991), pp. 304–14.

God has specially appointed me to this city, as though it was a large thoroughbred horse which because of its great size is inclined to be lazy and needs the stimulation of some stinging fly" (A, p. 16.). Living the way he did was fulfilling his duty to Athens. His life was not a matter of "minding his own business" in the sense that Pericles criticized. It was minding the business of Athens in precisely the way that was commanded by god. Private life – Socrates's way of living – was both fundamentally social and fulfilling his duty to Athens. How it was a way of minding the business of Athens needs explanation. The place to begin is with the ambiguity of Socrates's relationship to Athens as Plato represents it.

At the beginning of his defense in the *Apology*, Socrates begs the indulgence of his jurors for speaking to them in the manner he was accustomed to using at the marketplace. "This is my first appearance in a court of law, at the age of seventy, and so I am a complete stranger to the language of this place. Now if I were really from another country you would excuse me if I spoke in the manner and dialect in which I had been brought up" (A, p. 4.). While this suggestion that the jurors indulge Socrates as if he were a stranger served his purpose rhetorically, it is also typical of how Plato often has Socrates appear in the dialogues. Yet while Socrates may sometimes appear as a stranger to Athens, he also clearly affirms his loyalty. In the *Crito*, he tells Crito that he has a duty to Athens as a son to a parent, even to the extent of refusing to disobey her to save his life. Socrates, then, is represented by Plato as *both* stranger and citizen.

Werner Jaeger, in his monument of Greek cultural ideals, captured this ambiguity in a more fundamental way. "Socrates was one of the last citizens of the type which flourished in the earlier Greek polis. At the same time, he was the embodiment and the finest example of the new form of moral and intellectual individualism. Both these characters were united in him, without impairment of either."[24] Both stranger and citizen, both the old and the new morality joined without impairment in the person of Socrates.

How can that be so? In an unusually compelling interpretation of Socrates, Peter Euben provides a way of understanding the significance

[24] Werner Jaeger, *Paideia: Ideals of Greek Culture*, vol. II (Oxford: Oxford University Press, 1943), p. 75.

of this central ambiguity. Euben returns to Jaeger's interpretation, in particular Jaeger's curious suggestion that Achilles is actually the central figure of Plato's *Apology*. Achilles, it will be remembered, was to value honor even more than life in the *Iliad*. Yet when Odysseus encounters him in Hades in the *Odyssey* epic, Achilles expresses regret for that choice. Euben interprets Jaeger as meaning that "Achilles' relationship to the heroic ethic parallels Socrates' relationship to Athens. The former is at one and the same time the supreme embodiment of the heroic ethic and the one figure in the epic who comes closest to rejecting the ethic he embodies, while the latter is both the supreme embodiment and severest critic of Athenian tradition."[25]

Socrates's claim of unfamiliarity with the practices of the court allows him to hold Athens at arm's length, indicting Athens for trying him and claiming that its verdict condemns it, not him. Yet he submits to its judgment. He invokes its noble past, but offers the unconventionality of his own life as their salvation. He appeals to traditional Athenian ideals at the same time that he radicalizes them. Euben believes that Socrates's paradoxical relationship to Athens is the essential feature of his criticism. "His critical standards (including what it means to criticize on the basis of standards) are derived from what he criticizes . . . at least part of what is criticized is simultaneously affirmed."[26] Euben characterizes this tension between critic and citizen as the "tragic" element of Socrates, an element that is as significant as it is ignored by readers of the Socratic dialogues. What Euben means by the "tragic" is a critical position in relation to Athens that is both detached and embedded in the practices it casts into doubt. It is the deepest form of Socratic irony.

Scholars have made a great deal of Socratic irony – how it works and what it means for understanding Socrates. In common usage today, we take irony to be a kind of wry and distancing attitude, a kind of weary cleverness. But in its most straightforward meaning, irony is a rhetorical device in which what is meant is other than, and perhaps contrary to, what is actually said. Why would Socrates routinely employ such a rhetorical device? Was his intention to deceive his audience,

---

[25] J. Peter Euben, *The Tragedy of Political Theory: The Road Not Taken* (Princeton: Princeton University Press, 1990), pp. 220–1.
[26] *The Tragedy of Political Theory*, p. 230.

intentionally hiding his true meaning? Was he mocking them or having a joke at their expense? These hardly seem consistent with the moral aim of his discourse and his duty to Athens.

Gregory Vlastos has argued that prior to Socrates, irony may have been understood as a form of deception, but Socrates gave it a new form and meaning. For Vlastos, if we are to think of Socrates as only seeking the truth in his conversations with others, then his use of irony must be a sincere and honest way of conveying what he means to say. While the use of irony forces a burden on his audience to interpret what he says, his intended meaning must become transparent. In this sense, Socratic irony is no different in form from the now commonplace device of saying one thing to mean another. But it is different in that it is being employed for deeply moral reasons. "Socratic irony is not unique in accepting the burden of freedom which is inherent in all significant communication. It is unique in playing that game for bigger stakes than anyone else ever has in philosophy of the West."[27]

When Socrates resorts to irony, the stakes are high, and only irony is appropriate to the stakes. Socratic irony is, I think, what Euben means by the tragic and what I meant by the skeptical interpretation of Socrates in Chapter 2. Another way of putting it is that Socrates's position between what he says and what he means, or more generally, between the old and the new morality of Athens is structured by a certain kind of doubt – what I have called *deep doubt* – and a capacity to be both inside and outside the practices being doubted. His is the capacity to be between and hold in tension what is said and what is meant, the outside and the inside perspective, the conventional and the new. Irony serves to cast in doubt what is said by what is unsaid. The irony of the *Apology* joins the tragic and the skeptical, holding in a productive tension his own life and the life of Athens.

When Socrates claims that one who really cares about justice should live a private life and leave politics alone, and when this claim is situated in the context of what else we know about him, what seems ambivalent or ambiguous is better thought of as Socratic doubt of a deep and important sort. The point of discussing this tragic/ironic aspect of Socratic doubt is to recognize that private life for Socrates is not only a

[27] Gregory Vlastos, *Socrates: Ironist and Moral Philosopher* (Ithaca, NY: Cornell University Press, 1991), p. 44.

domain carved out against the *polis*. It is an essentially political project. Self-examination through dialogue in the marketplace was a form of political activity, albeit, of a fundamentally new form. By refusing to participate in the Assembly, and by refusing either to leave Athens or give up the practice of philosophy, he performed the greatest public service. Self-examination was one with continuous examination of the state.

Ironic ambivalence is at the very center of Socrates's doubt about public life. This ambivalence is not coincidental to skepticism. It is the political consequence of epistemological doubt. The enemy of skepticism first and foremost is dogmatism. Dogmatism is exemplified as much in the tyrannical opinions of the many that Socrates opposed as in the assertions of philosophers about reality opposed by followers of Pyrrho. Skeptical strategies against epistemological dogmatism incline one inward – toward self-examination for Socrates. Thus opposition to epistemological dogma fosters private life and the individual. But skepticism inclines one in the other direction as well. The political analog of epistemological opposition to dogmatism is opposition to violence. Skepticism was attractive, for example, to Montaigne, Locke, Hume, and even Kant because it tempered zealousness and favored an attitude of widening tolerance. In this respect, skepticism favored order and stability at the same time that it fostered a more individual outlook. The desire for order inclines one outward, to an accommodation with traditional, customary values and institutions.

The accommodation is ironic at best, however, simultaneously despising and needing the public realm and the requirements of public life. Socrates could condemn the opinion of the many yet argue in the *Crito* that one must persuade his Athenian jurors or obey the law of Athens. Montaigne, as we shall see in the Chapter 4, could ridicule customary practices and public demands yet favor existing institutions over revolutionary innovations. This skeptical, ironic stance toward public and private life – a stance of critical detachment on the one hand, and accommodation on the other – is well suited to our own ambivalence about public and private life detailed in the first part of this chapter. Let me suggest how.

Robert Bellah and his associates remark, at one point in their study of the corrosive affects of individualism in American life, on the oddness of the phrase *private citizen*, as if to suggest that it is self-contradictory. And I suggested as much, earlier, in reference to Pericles. Socrates's way of living, however, is an example of private citizenship. But it is a form of private citizenship importantly different from some ways that might be construed in contemporary discussion. Contrasting Socrates with two recent examples of what private citizenship might mean will make this point. In the introduction to *Contingency, Irony and Solidarity*, Richard Rorty writes that his book "tries to show how things look if we drop the demand for a theory which unifies the public and private, and are content to treat the demands of self-creation and of human solidarity as equally valid, yet forever incommensurable."[28] The private citizen this suggests is the one who can live simultaneously in two different worlds, the world of the study where poetry reigns and the public world defined by the requirements of procedural justice. It is a bifurcated life and irony provided the passage between the private and public parts.

Jean Elshtain offers a different reconstruction. Her way is to enrich private life with a sense of public responsibility while recasting public institutions in ways that nurture private life. She puts it this way:

Such a world would require private spheres bearing their own intrinsic dignity and purposes tied to moral and aesthetic imperative, all the textures, nuances, tones and touches of a life lived intimately among others. A richly complex private sphere requires, in order that it survive, freedom from some all-encompassing public imperative, but in order for it to flourish the public world itself must nurture and sustain a set of ethical imperatives, including a commitment to preserve, protect, and defend human beings in their capacities as private persons, and to allow men and women alike to partake in the good of the public sphere on an equal basis of participatory dignity and equality. Rather than an ideal of citizenship and civic virtue that features a citizenry grimly going about their collective duty, or an elite band of citizens in their "public space" cut off from a world that includes most of the rest of us, within the ethical polity the active citizen would be one who had affirmed as part of what it meant to be fully human a devotion to public, moral responsibility.[29]

Elshtain understands the importance of private life for freedom, and she appreciates the fullness of its constitution in relations of intimacy.

---

[28] Richard Rorty, *Contingency, Irony and Solidarity* (Cambridge: Cambridge University Press, 1989), p. xv.
[29] *Public Man and Private Woman*, p. 351.

Her reconstruction seeks to recast the public and private by infusing each with the other. While Rorty seeks to achieve peaceful coexistence, Elshtain seeks both a mutually supporting relationship between the two and preservation of a tension between public and private spheres as a way of resisting the powerful danger that the polity will overwhelm the individual.

The Socratic conception that I have sketched shares Elshtain's sense of the richness of private life in contrast to Rorty's aestheticized and individualistic conception and in contrast to the self-absorbed tendencies of modern culture that Bellah and his colleagues worry about. In contrast to Elshtain, the Socratic conception shares Rorty's skepticism about the public world, not expecting public institutions to nurture and sustain private flourishing. But the deep doubt of Socrates – as distinct from Rorty's – is a form of doubt through which we inhabit public practices in new and transforming ways, not simply the way of negotiating Rorty's gulf between the poet and the citizen. The point of Socratic doubt is to maintain and heighten the tension between care of the soul and the public world. *Private citizen* seems exactly the right phrase to capture the politics of skepticism I have attributed to Socrates. This sort of politics, I believe, implies an ongoing contest over crucial issues of public concern – such as those that animate feminist critique – while, also maintaining private life as the place of freedom and as the lever for criticism of the public institutions. And more, it is true to an aspect of contemporary culture concealed by critics' preoccupation with the modern tendency toward self-absorption. Preserving relations of intimacy through which we come to know ourselves through others is as often the outcome of skepticism about the public and political as is narcissistic individualism.

Socrates's god called him to a life of self-examination, a life conducted in the marketplace, at the banquet, and on the road. This was a calling of the highest civic duty, one he was willing to give his life for. Socratic doubt calls forth a form of private life through which he joined the project of individual authenticity, the bonds of intimacy among friends, and duty to the *polis*. The deeply ironic nature of his doubt casts him as both insider and outsider to the claims of the public world. The tension set up and sustained by his deep doubt is as politically productive as it is personally therapeutic, contributing at the same time to private well-being and to civic duty. It offers the capacity to transform the cynical implications of our skepticism about public institutions into productive criticism. More than that, it suggests to us that it is the *maintenance* of the tension between the demands of private and public life, not the *resolution* of that tension, that is likely to foster both private freedom and public responsibility. To be a citizen in a democracy is to be able to live effectively with that tension.

4

Doubt and Conviction

The liberal societies of our century have produced more and more people who are able to recognize the contingency of the vocabularies in
which they state their highest hopes – the contingency of their consciences – and yet remain faithful to those consciences.

Richard Rorty, *Contingency, Irony and Solidarity*[1]

The political philosopher Isaiah Berlin made famous a line from
Joseph Schumpeter: "To realize the relative validity of one's convictions and yet stand for them unflinchingly is what distinguishes a civilized man from a barbarian."[2] But this is exactly what some social critics
would deny. Doubt about the validity of one's convictions breeds relativism and relativism is the enemy of what is best about our culture,
it is claimed. The most bombastic of them is William Bennett, whom I
quoted in Chapter 1: "In living memory the chief threats to America
Democracy have come from without: first, Nazism and Japanese imperialism, and later, Soviet communism. But these wars, hot or cold,
ended in spectacular American victories. The threats we now face are
from within. They are far different, more difficult to detect, and more
insidious: decadence, cynicism, and boredom."[3] Bennett traces these

---

[1] Richard Rorty, *Contingency, Irony and Solidarity* (Cambridge: Cambridge University
Press, 1989), p. 46.
[2] Isaiah Berlin, *Four Essays on Liberty* (Oxford: Oxford University Press, 1969), p. 172.
[3] William J. Bennett, *The Death of Outrage: Bill Clinton and the Assault on American Ideals*
(New York: The Free Press, 1998), p. 130.

threats to a culture of self-doubt and relativism. This is what Jeffrey Goldfarb takes to be the source of cynicism in American life: "When we no longer know that our way of life is best, we learn to respect others, but we also learn to doubt ourselves. Our positions on political, social, and even religious issues come to appear accidental, more the product of who we are – our class position, nationality, and limited interests – than a product of how we think and act. Thus the quality of what we say and do come to be understood cynically."[4] And Michael Sandel takes it to be one of the consequences of liberalism that is not only the source of democracy's discontent, it undermines the very values liberals espouse. Responding directly to Berlin and Berlin's use of Schumpeter, Sandel claims that "if one's convictions are only relatively valid, why stand for them unflinchingly? In a tragically configured moral universe, such as Berlin assumes, is the ideal of freedom any less subject than competing ideals to the ultimate incommensurability of values? If so, in what can its privileged status consist? And if freedom has no morally privileged status, if it is just one value among many, then what can be said for liberalism?"[5]

Can one live with both fundamental doubts and deep conviction as Schumpeter suggest? I have suggested in earlier chapters that to do so is central to the democratic personality, especially if we are to think about democracy in terms of authentic deliberation among citizens. But is this a responsible way to live? Social conservatives are not alone in claiming that it is not. There are two aspects to these questions that I want to consider. One is directed at the possibility of living with the kind of deep self-doubt that I claim was characteristic of the type of democratic citizenship I attribute to Socrates. Can we act purposefully and live in good faith and at the same time harbor fundamental doubts about the basis upon which we live and act? Can we live effectively with deep doubt? Of course one can live with doubts. We always live with doubts. Can doubt – of the fundamental sort that Socrates or the Pyrrhonian skeptics raised – be an effective and responsible strategy for living? At the level of conduct, the question is this: Can we have both

4 Jeffrey C. Goldfarb, *The Cynical Society: The Culture of Politics and the Politics of Culture in American Life* (Chicago: University of Chicago Press, 1991), p. 10.
5 Michael Sandel, *Liberalism and its Critics* (New York: New York University Press, 1984), p. 8.

deep doubt and moral or political conviction? The other aspect of the question is more theoretical and is directed at the possibility of social or political critique on the basis of our moral or political convictions if those convictions are subject to doubt. Can criticism that recognizes the contingency of the vocabulary in which it expresses its highest hopes – in Rorty's phrase – be politically effective or does it undercut the very possibility of political criticism?

So far as conduct is concerned I think conviction requires a willingness to act not an unwillingness to doubt. As I suggested, at least that is what characterized Socrates's brand of skepticism. All the while professing ignorance in fundamental matters, he was willing to die – he did die – for his convictions. Yet even up to the hour of his death, he was willing to open them up again and reexamine the convictions that led him to his death sentence. It seems to me a betrayal of Socrates's courage to explain this as evidence that he must have really had moral certainty despite his protestations to the contrary. The Socratic way of life is exemplary not because he was certain but because he wasn't; and still he acted with conviction. As I suggested in Chapter 3, Montaigne appreciated this aspect of Socrates, and I will use Montaigne as a more systematic case study of a life that combined fundamental doubts with unflinching conviction.

The issue of political discourse that doubts its deepest convictions is a bit different. It is implied in Sandel's criticism of liberalism that I quoted in the preceding text. On Sandel's view, liberalism's commitment to "values pluralism" undercuts the very possibility of political critique because its central value – freedom – must be among the plurality of values. If freedom is ungrounded, then it is unclear how one can criticize political regimes in the name of expanding freedom. A similar argument has been made against the arguably illiberal social theorist Michel Foucault. Some would argue that his analyses of modern social institutions and claims about the ubiquity of power undercut any political critique that could liberate us from the mechanisms of power he so compellingly identified. This has been the charge against Foucault made by Jurgen Habermas and Charles Taylor, for example.

In his works on social institutions and the emergence of modern forms of power, Foucault opposed, in two crucial respects, the way we have thought about political power since the seventeeth century. First, it has been central to the liberal political tradition since Loeke and Condorcet to think of power as opposed to knowledge, suppressing and distorting it in the way that tyrants suppress individuals. By contrast Foucault claimed that power could not exist in the absence of knowledge nor knowledge in the absence of power. As readers of Foucault know, he captured this interdependence of power and knowledge by juxtaposing them in his writing as "power/knowledge." Second, and in contrast to Enlightenment thought, which views the role of knowledge in politics as providing freedom from power through a critique of political regimes, Foucault claimed that there were no power-free relations from which to criticize political institutions and to which one might be liberated. Furthermore, he claimed that the idea that there are evaluative criteria independent of particular power/knowledge regimes upon which critique depends, was just one of the ways that modern power manifests itself.[6] Though his analysis is subtle and complex, this is enough to suggest the problem posed by recognizing the contingency of our practices and denying that there is anything more fundamental outside of them.

If there are no power-free relations and there are no independent criteria upon which to evaluate and oppose power regimes, what is the status of Foucault's own political discourse so far as current social conditions are concerned?[7] His rhetoric leaves no doubt that he despises the forms of discipline, supervision, regulation, and normalizing power that characterize modern social institutions. Yet his deepest critics have argued that Foucault's political discourse is self-defeating because he rejects those very features of Enlightenment and modernity – truth and freedom – that make social criticism possible. Thus, it is claimed, he eliminates the possibility that his own writing could be politically effective.[8] Contrary to his rhetoric, his work cannot avoid acquiesing in the very institutions and values of the current power regime that he so clearly despises.

[6] Michel Foucault, *Power/Knowledge: Selected Interviews and Other Writings*, Colin Gordon, ed. (New York: Pantheon Books, 1980).
[7] Richard Bernstein, "Foucault: Critique as a Philosophical Ethos," *The New Constellation* (Cambridge, MA: MIT Press, 1992).
[8] See Jurgen Habermas, *Philosophical Discourse of Modernity* (Cambridge, MA: MIT Press, 1987) and Charles Taylor, "Foucault on Freedom and Truth," in *Philosophical Papers*, *Vol.* 2 (Cambridge: Cambridge University Press, 1987).

This charge against Foucault has also been brought against Jacques Derrida, and more recently, against Richard Rorty.[9] I want to extend it, however, as a problem that arises for political discourse generally in the aftermath of the recent antifoundationalist and interpretive turn that political philosophy has taken. If, as is the case with Foucault, Rorty, and Derrida, interpretation of social institutions is not grounded in truth, rationality, or some such and if our political values are contingent, then how can we do anything more than articulate and reproduce the values currently circulating in society or lash out at those values arbitarily? If one abandons political theorizing in the traditional sense, how can this sort of political writing have political content? How can it avoid a pernicious skepticism on the one hand or a debilitating conservatism on the other? If recent political discourse aspires to serious criticism of current values and institutions, how can its critique be more than arbitrary? How can such writing serve the aims of social and political life? What is the political status of skeptically motivated discourse?

Montaigne, perhaps more than any other author, was acutely aware of both the challenge of living with doubt and conviction and the problem posed by the political purposes of his own writing. So I will use him as a case study to consider these questions. I think that an effort to appreciate the relationship between writing and politics in Montaigne's *Essays* will be repaid when we return to recent forms of political writing such as Foucault's that consciously depart from political theorizing.

Montaigne's *Essays* are not overtly political. If we are to believe Montaigne (an issue I will turn to shortly), they were intended merely to serve the private and domestic function of reminding his friends and relatives about himself. The hundred or so entries that make up the three books of the *Essays* were written and added to over a period of sixteen years resulting in a collage of observations about a wide variety of topics concerning such things as religion, character, custom, exemplary individuals, fashion, military action, antiquity, vanity, death, himself, and history. Through the course of these essays, he manages to cast doubt on most of what political philosophy seeks to justify. In

[9] See, for example, Jurgen Habermas, *Philosophical Discourse of Modernity* and Nancy Fraser, "Solidarity or Singularity: Richard Rorty between Romanticism and Technocracy," in *Reading Rorty,* Alan R Malachowiski, ed. (Oxford: Basil Blackwell, 1990).

particular, he is skeptical about human nature, reason, and truth that serve to ground political theory. The *Essays* present human beings as "a patchwork and a motley (E II: 20, 511)," reason as folly (E II: 12), and morals as disparate, variable, and relative (esp. E I: 23, 31, 36). Furthermore, while Montaigne pokes fun at existing social institutions, he does not recommend their reform. He claims to be "disgusted with innovation, in whatever guise . . . (E II: 23, 86)" and that would include political innovation. He opposed revolution and reform in favor of loyalty to customary and traditional values and institutions.

Because the *Essays* are destructive of the very foundations of political theory and the possibility of radical social reform, they might seem to some to constitute an antipolitics, in much the way Michel Foucault's critics have viewed his works on modern power as antipolitical. But they are not . . . or so I shall argue. Regarding the reading of Montaigne that I propose, the positive aim of the *Essays* is to exhibit possibilities for social life in the *absence* of fundamental political certainties and without an overt reformist outlook about existing social conditions and institutions.

David Lewis Schaefer's *The Political Philosophy of Montaigne* is among the very few studies of Montaigne that seek to present him as a systematic political philosopher. Schaefer claims that it was Montaigne who laid the foundations for modern liberalism.[10] His is the most thorough discussion of the relationship between Montaigne's skepticism and his politics to date, and while there is a great deal in his study that I agree with, I will end up taking issue with Schaefer at several key points. I depart from Schaefer's interpretation in two ways. First, Schaefer does not think that ancient skepticism offers a positive possibility for political life whereas I shall, both in my interpretation of Socrates and the Pyrrhonian skeptics, argue that it does. Second, and related, he thinks that because Montaigne does offer a positive politics he is not a skeptic after all. I, however, take Montaigne to be the prototype of the politics of skepticism.

It is a matter of scholarly controversy as to the degree to which Montaigne's interest in skepticism, particularly Pyrrhonism, was a passing phase in Montaigne's influence and whether it or Stoicism was

[10] David Lewis Schaefer, *The Political Philosophy of Montaigne* (Ithaca, NY: Cornell University Press, 1990).

more significant for Montaigne's mature thought. Many of his earliest interpreters – Pascal and Bayle, for example – knew primarily Montaigne's most skeptical essay, "Apology for Raymond Sebond," and they took him to be an extreme Pyrrhonist. However, Donald Frame, among the best English translators and interpreters of the *Essays,* has placed greater weight on the stoical aspects of the *Essays,* claiming that skepticism was a passing enthusiasm. Schaefer has argued effectively that Pyrrhonism is central to the *Essays* but he thinks that Montaigne departs from skepticism because it is entirely negative and he believes that Montaigne intended to offer a positive politics. I think Schaefer is right about the positive thrust of Montaigne's politics but contrary to Schaefer, I think this shows how it is that fundamental doubts of the sort that Montaigne entertained allow for both personal conviction and positive political criticism.

It is well-known that Montaigne was greatly influenced by Sextus Empiricus's *Outlines of Pyrrhonism* at a strategic period in the development of the *Essays.* Montaigne had painted on the ceiling of his library the line from Sextus, "To any reason an equal reason can be opposed." His personal medallion was of balanced scales representing skeptical equilibrium. His longest essay, "Apology for Raymond Sebond" employed arguments from Sextus in what, in anyone's estimate, is a very ironic defense of Sebond's natural theology. What I want to address, however, is how, taken together, the *Essays* answer to the charge that a Pyrrhonian politics is self-defeating. That is, I am not concerned, as Schaefer is, with the place of Pyrrhonism in Montaigne's thought so much as with Montaigne's place in the tradition of the politics of skepticism. Montaigne's "solution" to the problem of Pyrrhonism transforms skepticism by representing its potential for positive politics. He offers a portrait of a skeptical but active life, which, while not reformist, is also not politically acquiescent.

Any political reading of the *Essays* must come to terms with Montaigne's paradoxical preface to his reader. It is so important that I quote it in full.

This book was written in good faith, reader. It warns you from the outset that in it I have set myself no goal but a domestic and private one. I have no thought of serving either you or my own glory. My powers are inadequate for such a purpose. I have dedicated it to the private convenience of my relatives and friends, so that when they have lost me (as soon they must), they may recover here some features of my habits and temperament, and by this means keep the knowledge they have had of me more complete and alive.

If I had written to seek the world's favor, I should have bedecked myself better and should present myself in a studied posture. I want to be seen here in my simple, natural, ordinary fashion, without straining or artifice; for it is myself that I portray. My defects will here be read to the life, and also my natural form, as far as respect for the public has allowed. Had I been placed among those nations which are said to live still in the sweet freedom of nature's first laws, I assure you I should very gladly have portrayed myself here entire and wholly naked. Thus, reader, I am myself the matter of my book, you would be unreasonable to spend your leisure on so frivolous and vain a subject (E I, 2).

A great deal has been made of the ironic warning of the preface and what it foretells about the essays that follow. If we take the preface seriously and if the essays that follow are written in good faith, then we should not expect to find anything in them of political interest or public benefit. Yet throughout the essays that follow, Montaigne constantly interrupted particular observations with explanations about the nature of his work, his ideal readership, and the benefit of what he is doing. Furthermore, though Montaigne was indeed the subject of his book, he was so in no ordinary way. The book is not about Montaigne's life in the same way that the *Confessions* were about Rousseau's. And it is in no way a series of recollections for the private convenience of his intimates in any usual sense. Put another way, in so far as it was addressed to his intimates, the serious reader of the *Essays* must be counted among them.

Though Montaigne purported to write in a simple and natural fashion, without straining and artifice, the individual essays generously quote classic sources – usually without attribution – and the structure of the work as a whole is artificial at best. The attentive reader, however, cannot conclude that because the work turns out to be of serious value beyond Montaigne's modest claims for it, Montaigne dissimulates. One of the more frequent themes of the work – a theme that was to influence Rousseau's *First Discourse* and *Emile* later – is Montaigne's disgust at society in which dissimulation, masks, the adoption of social roles, and the vanity of words had become the norm for public life. If he dissimulates, then he is merely reproducing the form of life he despises in the essays.

What then, are we to make of the preface and the public purpose of the essays that follow? There are three parts to the answer. Two are connected directly with the problem Pyrrhonism faces in offering skepticism as a way of life. The third has to do with his conception of the public and private spheres that extends the Socratic interpretation I offered in Chapter 3.

The first part of the answer turns on the standard point that the essay – which Montaigne invented – is a form of writing ideally suited to Montaigne's Pyrrhonian outlook because, as efforts or experiments, the essay always remain tentative and undogmatic in presentation. Montaigne observed that "If my mind could gain a firm footing, I would not make essays, I would make decisions..." (E II: 2, 611). Where nothing is certain and secure one can only make experimental attempts.

The connection between skepticism and the essay form of writing is reinforced in various ways in the work. The lack of any formal or theoretical framework to bind the individual essays together as a coherent whole; the sometimes lack of connection between an essay's title and its content; the lack within certain of the essays – especially the later ones – of a discernible connection between paragraphs and even between sentences; the contradictions and constant cataloging of positions and their opposites; the "overwriting" and insertion of new material into the essays over a period of years without revising earlier material: all of these rhetorical techniques serve to *show* what Pyrrhonism could not assert without refuting itself. Even when the subject of an essay doubts truth or knowledge, the form of the writing, rather than claims that are made, carries the burden of the skepticism. The "Apology for Raymond Sebond" does not argue for its skeptical stance so much as it shows it in waves of juxtaposition, citation, aside, ad hominem, and table banging. Finally, by making himself the subject of his book Montaigne could record the shifting play of appearances, events, issues, and experiences as they caught his fancy. In so doing, the essays remained always open-ended, always recording only how things appeared to him at the moment. In essaying himself, he could present his skepticism without dogmatism.

But Montaigne's warning to the reader in his preface reveals not only how conscious he was of the rhetorical status of his own writing, it reveals how conscious he was of the interpretive task that is placed on his reader. This is the second part of answering the question about the public purpose of the *Essays*. In making himself the subject of his book, Montaigne can be read as a model of the Pyrrhonian way of life. The picture he painted of himself was of someone who is constantly shifting and changing and at the same time conscious of the power of habit and steadfast in his commitment to his traditional values. But in writing the way he did, he was not simply offering up the results of his attempts at observing himself for a passive audience. The attentive reader – warned by the preface and by Montaigne's numerous remarks about his ideal reader – is forced to recognize himself or herself in the text. Pascal observed that when he went to the *Essays* to find Montaigne, he found himself instead.

In an excellent study, Terence Cave has worked out with considerable care the dynamic relationship between Montaigne as writer and rewriter of the *Essays*, Montaigne's own reading of other authors, and the demands Montaigne places on the reader of the *Essays*. Cave concludes that this relationship between writing and reading moves the *Essays* – and consequently Montaigne's claim to be writing only about himself – beyond the writer's control: "[T]he image of [Montaigne's] self-portrait now begins to dissolve, since the perfect reader is the one who, in following the traces of self-portrait and understanding their function, learns that whatever of value he is to gain from the text must be organized in terms of his own experience, not Montaigne's ... The text remains perpetually an open question; the reader embarks on an endless quest."[11] Cave's point in my terms is that the Pyrrhonian practice is carried by the activity of reading as well as Montaigne's writing, or perhaps better, by the tension that the *Essays* sets up between its writer and reader. Reading is a form of essaying. As a result, one not only reads Montaigne in the *Essays*, one becomes author of oneself. Reading the essays is a transforming activity.

There is more to the relationship between the writer and reader of the *Essays* than this, however. In accepting Montaigne's claim in the preface to be writing only for his intimates, the *Essays* invite a relationship of intimacy to begin between the reader and Montaigne.

---

[11] Terence Cave, "Problems of Reading in the *Essays*," in *Michel de Montaigne: Modern Critical Views*, Harold Bloom, ed. (New York: Chelsea House Publishers, 1987), p. 114.

And this introduces the third part of my answer to the question about the political status of Montaigne's writing. This part of the answer turns on the views of private and public life that are revealed there.

Montaigne's essay "Of Repentance" – one of many where he reflects on the nature of the essay – is a useful place to initiate the point I wish to develop. In it, Montaigne addressed the issue of the inconsistences in his essays. He wrote:

> the lines of my painting do not go astray, though they change and vary. The world is but a perennial movement. All things in it are in constant motion.
>
> . . . I do not portray being: I portray passing. Not the passing from one age to another, or, as the people say, for seven years to seven years, but from day to day, from minute to minute. . . . This is a record of various and changeable occurrences, and of irresolute and, when it so befalls, contradictory ideas. . . . If my mind could gain a firm footing, I would not make essays, I would make decisions; but it is always in apprenticeship and on trial.
>
> Authors communicate with the people by some special extrinsic mark; I am the first to do so by my entire being, as Michel de Montaigne, not as a grammarian or a poet or a jurist. If the world complains that I speak too much of myself, I complain that it does not even think of itself.
>
> But is it reasonable that I, so fond of privacy in actual life, should aspire to publicity in the knowledge of me (E III: 2, 610–611)?

This passage provides a useful summary of the skeptical themes I have been addressing: the Pyrrhonian appreciation of change and appearance, the rationale for the essay form, the complex relationship between writer and reader, and Montaigne as a model for a Pyrrhonian way of life against which the reader must test himself or herself. But to move beyond Pyrrhonian interpretation to skeptical politics – to a specific political content – I wish to focus on the final question of the passage: Is it reasonable that he, Montaigne, so fond of private life as he is, should aspire for publicity of himself?

The issue behind this question is not whether one who claims only to be engaged in a domestic and private project for his family and intimates should wish to make his book public. Rather, it is the nature of private and public life and their relationship that the question opens up for essay. The model of private and public life that flows from the *Essays* should be read, I think, in terms of the complex interpretive relationship that exists between the particulars of

Montaigne's own life, the rhetorical problem of the *Essays*, and its political implications.

To begin with Montaigne, it is significant to know that he had been an active participant in public life, twice serving as the mayor of Bordeaux and claiming membership in the "nobility of the sword." But he quit his public duties and withdrew to his estate and to his library to essay himself. His seventeeth- and eighteenth-century interpreters criticized him for indolence and self-indulgence, taking this retreat to his chateau and the literal claims of his preface as their evidence.[12] On some recent interpretations, on Jean Starobinski's for example, his retreat into himself was the result of his disillusionment with the public sphere.[13] By retreating he could achieve a proper distance from it to observe its follies and express his disgust. I shall claim, however, that the circumstances of Montaigne's retreat to his chateau and the essays that resulted suggest that his understanding of the public sphere and his turn toward private life is similar to Socrates both in the way he held together deep doubt and strong conviction, and in the way that he constructed a tension between private life and political criticism.

I argued in Chapter 3 that our concepts of a public and a private sphere are confused. One reason for the confusion is the fact that in the history of the concepts quite different things have been at stake philosophically. Different features of the public and private have been taken as essential and epistemological concepts, such as incorrigibility, or political concepts, such as freedom, are located differently as a result. A related reason for confusion is the fact that the contrast between public and private is more normative than descriptive because the line one draws establishes an evaluative hierarchy. Thus, the concepts are "essentially contested" in that attempts to define and set the boundaries between and disagreements about such attempts are inevitably part of political controversies that are open and ongoing.[14] This has become clearer to us recently because of feminists' arguments

---

[12] Arthur Augustus Tilley, "Montaigne's Interpreters," *Studies in French Renaissance* (Cambridge: Cambridge University Press, 1922).

[13] Jean Starobinski, *Montaigne in Motion* (Chicago: University of Chicago Press, 1985), pp. 6–7.

[14] For a fuller discussion of "essentially contested concepts" see William E. Connolly, *The Terms of Political Discourse*, 2nd ed. (Princeton: Princeton University Press, 1983).

against liberal conceptions of the private as well as their opposition to legal and legislative decisions about such "domestic" issues as spouse abuse, abortion, and support for child care.[15]

In a useful recent analysis, Hanna Pitkin has suggested three dimensions along which the public and private are now conceived: (1) the public as accessible to all in contrast with the reserved, closed, or hidden; (2) that which affects all as opposed to the personal; and (3) public direction or control in contrast to private interests.[16] Her formulation nicely frames the varied historical sources from which our modern conception of privacy derives. From Descartes, for example, the notion of the private as hidden takes on a sense of inwardness, and this is for primarily metaphysical and epistemological reasons. The private is the interior, subjective realm of the individual, the mark of consciousness and the seat of certainty. From Kant's ethics the private takes on the sense of the personal and partial in contrast to the generality of our moral imperatives. From Rousseau the private gets the sense of self-control or self-dependency, *amour de soi* as distinct from the corrupt form of self-love that he denoted by *amour propre.*

What each of these modern notions has in common is an identification of the private with something about the individual's relationship to himself. As a result, the private has been constructed not only in opposition to the public but also in opposition to the social, as an opposition between an individual and others. This is implied by liberal attempts to construct social values by aggregating "private interests" of essentially asocial individuals, and it is implied by communitarian charges that such attempts cannot succeed in establishing a strong sense of communal values. My reason for sketching these modern conceptions is to highlight, by contrast, the picture of private life that one reads in the *Essays.* This picture can be brought into focus by considering, first, what Montaigne suggests about public life. What one finds is a notion of public as audience, as the sphere one enters as actor. As such, we are truly not ourselves in the public arena. We put on masks and adopt social roles. We flatter and cultivate the opinion of others. As I shall

---

[15] See, for example, Carole Pateman, "Feminist Critiques of the Public/Private Dichotomy," in *Public and Private in Social Life*, pp. 281–303.

[16] Hanna Fenichel Pitkin, "Justice: On Relating Private and Public," *Political Theory*, vol. 9, 1981, pp. 329–30

suggest in Chapter 5, this is the sense of public that was to influence Rousseau's *First Discourse*. But whereas Rousseau was to withdraw from the deceits of the public world into himself to write solitary reveries, Montaigne withdrew to his chateau and his friends to essay himself for their benefit.

In "Of Repentance" Montaigne was concerned with the ease with which one can adopt a public role compared with the difficulty of ordering one's private life. "It is a rare life," Montaigne wrote, "that remains well ordered even in private. Any man can play his part in the side show and represent a worthy man on the boards; but to be disciplined within, in his own bosom, where all is permissible, where all is concealed – that is the point," (E III: 2, 613). This theme of the overriding need for a well-ordered private life is joined to the claim, in his essay "Of Husbanding Your Will," that one's duty to oneself is a priority over service to others. "[T]he passions that distract me from myself and attach me elsewhere, those in truth I oppose with all my strength. My opinion is that we must lend ourselves to others and give ourselves only to ourselves" (E III: 10, 767).

The point of reforming private life and remaining loyal to oneself is that one might, thereby, achieve tranquility and repose but this is not in lieu of public duty. In the essay "On Husbanding Your Will," Montaigne pointed to his own experiences as mayor of Bordeaux to discuss the connection between private repose and public duty.

This man, knowing exactly what he owes to himself, finds it in his part that he is to apply to himself his experiences of other men and of the world, and, in order to do so contribute to public society the duties and services within his province. He who lives not at all unto others, hardly lives unto himself. He who is a friend to himself, know that that man is a friend to all [Seneca].

. . . I do not want a man to refuse, to the charges he takes on, attention, steps words, and sweat and blood if need be. . . . But this is by way of loan and accidentally, the mind holding itself ever in repose and in health, not without action, but without vexation, without passion. (E III: 10, 769–70)

Though care of private life is the priority, private and public life are interdependent. The private repose that skepticism makes possible provides the most effective means of performing one's public roles, of living with the ambiguity of the public world, and of audience, appearance, and contingency.

The second thing that prevents private life from inwardness and quietude is Montaigne's more expansive conception of privacy, one connected to intimacy rather than inwardness. My discussion of public and private life was introduced many pages earlier as part of an answer to this question: What are we to make of the public purpose of the *Essays* given that Montaigne has said in the preface that they were merely about himself for his intimates? From Montaigne's conception of the public sphere, it follows that he can only reveal himself as he is and without masks in private to his intimates; thus the *Essays* construct not a public, not an audience, but a friendship. The dialectic that the preface sets up between Montaigne and his reader invites the reader to become an intimate. Read this way, Montaigne is "the matter of his book" in the way that a friend reveals himself to a friend. The reader becomes intimate with Montaigne by sharing in all of the various fragmented incidents, experiences, shifting observations, and contradictions through which anyone befriends another. Our private life is the sphere in which we reveal ourselves as we are to our friends: not the Cartesian sphere in which we reveal ourselves incorrigibly to ourselves alone, but a relationship with others in which we are revealed through all the transitory and contingent experiences that form "the patchwork" that is our self.

In the essay "Of Friendship" Montaigne cited with approval Aristotle's remark that "good legislators have had more care for friendship than for justice (E I: 28, 136)." Though the essay distinguished real friendship – the model being his friendship with Etienne de la Boetie in which "our souls mingle and blend with each other so completely that they efface the seam that joined them" (E I:28, 139) – from more common forms of friendship, there are two features of even common friendships that are significant for my purpose. First, the relationship of friend to friend is one of irreducible mutuality. That is, it cannot be reduced to merely the coupling of individual interests. "[T]here are no dealings or business except with itself" (E I:28, 138). It cannot be decomposed into the independent interests and intentions of the individuals involved. If privacy is construed as intimacy and the basis of intimacy is friendship, privacy is not individualistic, subjective, or inward. Already, the private is more expansive and richer than our modern version, embracing friends, family, and loved ones.

Second, it is in the intimacy of friendship that we do not need to play a part or to put on masks. Because the relationship between Montaigne and his reader is drawn in contrast to the public relationship between actor and audience, the preface to the *Essays* establishes this conception of privacy – not withdrawal into oneself or retreat to the library, but instead, the sphere in which one is truly oneself among one's intimates. As such, care for private life takes priority over all else because it is only there that one can aspire to a well-ordered life.

This notion of the priority of private life constitutes one source for Montaigne's distrust of reformers and revolutionaries – distrust that has led critics to characterizing him as politically conservative. In "Of Repentance," he writes:

Those who in my time have tried to correct the world's morals by new ideas reform the superficial vices; the essential ones they leave as they were, if they do not increase them and increase is to be feared. People are likely to rest from all other well-doing on the strength of those external, arbitrary reforms, which cost us less and bring greater acclaim, and thereby they satisfy at little expense the other natural, consubstantial, and internal vices. (E III: 2, 616)

Here and throughout the *Essays* Montaigne observes the various ways in which we become enslaved by the superficial requirements of public life to the neglect of ourselves, with the result that our public lives are mere busyness.

Montaigne's Pyrrhonism does not entail busyness, public inactivity, and retreat into one's self or a bifurcated life that adheres to one standard in private and another in public. Rather, the private repose that skepticism brings about is the most effective means for acting in the public world of contingency, uncertainty, and appearances. This leads to a final point having to do with Montaigne's apparent opposition to social and political reform.

Private repose cannot be publicly effective if it implies uncritical acquiescence in the status quo, and that is precisely what some of Montaigne's critics have charged. I suggested previously that Montaigne distrusted innovators and reformers because they sought to change superficial public vices rather than private values. There is another, related reason that has to do with his distrust of political principles generally. It is in terms of this that we can confront the charge that a politics of skepticism is conservatism. I shall approach the issue by way of his essay, "Of Freedom of Conscience." The point I wish to establish is that skeptical opposition on epistemological grounds to metaphysical claims about reality is mirrored in Montaigne's opposition on utilitarian grounds to reformers who wish to change the existing order on the basis of political principle. Both are opposed to dogmatism, but the form dogmatism took in the eyes of the Pyrrhonian skeptics was philosophy. The form it takes for Montaigne is violence. Making this point through the essay, "Of Freedom of Conscience," is tricky, however, so I need to qualify what follows.

The rhetorical effect of Montaigne's essays favors and fosters toleration. Schaefer has done an admirable job of developing this aspect of Montaigne. Skepticism has often served to underwrite a commitment to tolerance. That was the case with Locke and with Kant.[17] But tolerance as a trait of mind is quite different from tolerance as a political principle, and skepticism and toleration are linked for pragmatic rather than principled considerations. This is the point to be made for Montaigne.

"Of Freedom of Conscience" began with an observation about the Protestant Reformation: "In this controversy on whose account France is at present agitated by civil wars, the best and soundest side is undoubtedly that which maintains both the old religion and the old government" (E II: 19, 506). Though this observation seems merely to justify the claim that Montaigne was a political conservative, he undermined the apparent conservatism by detailing, in the essay, the equal danger of violent excess posed by the zealous defenders of the old religion and the old government. He made the point by juxtaposing the case of Emperor Julian and the current situation of religious turmoil in France. In contrast to Christian hostility to Julian, Montaigne offered a portrait of him as a "very great and rare man" to be admired for his sense of justice, sobriety, philosophical patience, military ability, and manner of facing his own death (E II: 19, 507). It is worth noticing that Montaigne admires both his repose and his active life.

---

[17] See Richard Tuck, "Scepticism and Toleration in the Seventeenth Century," in *Justifying Toleration*, Susan Mendus, ed. (Cambridge: Cambridge University Press, 1988); J. C. Laurensen, "Scepticism and Intellectual Freedom: The Philosophical Foundations of Kant's Polities of Publicity," *History of Political Thought*, vol. 10 1989; and Richard Rorty, *Contingency, Irony and Solidarity* (Cambridge: Cambridge University Press, 1988).

Montaigne criticized Julian, however, because he dissembled in his own religious beliefs and supported religious freedom to foster schisms and factions. Schaefer argues that Montaigne's intent in "Of Freedom of Conscience" is deeply antireligious and that he, like Julian, wishes to destroy Christianity. My interpretation is somewhat different.

The discussion of Julian shows, I think, how toleration could as easily be used in the service of fostering dissensions as in relieving them. This characteristically Pyrrhonian strategy of opposing claims for freedom of conscience with their opposite effects undermines reformist confidence in the validity of toleration as a fulcrum for social critique. The skeptic would employ a similar strategy against other political principles. The point is that zealousness and unyielding certainty in the name of principle destabilizes the social order. Stability, so far as possible, is to be maintained. As the beginning of the essay shows, Montaigne favored the old religion, but he favored it for its social utility in the current turmoil, not because of any authority conveyed to it by time. At the same time, however, he employed the same Pyrrhonian strategy to undermine claims for customary and traditional values. The result is a politics that seeks to remain loyal to the customary public values for reasons of stability without rendering them immune to criticism and change. That is the theme of the essay, "Of Custom, and Not Easily Changing an Accepted Law."

"Of Custom" begins with remarks on the tenacity of habit, the difficulty of changing habits, and the importance of instilling good habits in childhood. To make the point about the power of habit, Montaigne asked: "Is there any opinion so bizarre ... that habit has not planted and established it by law in the regions where she saw fit to do so?" (E I: 23, 79). There follows page after page of bizarre practices that are customary in some country, each juxtaposed with opposite practices in another. The conclusion he drew was that "there is nothing that custom will not or cannot do" (E I: 23, 83). As you would expect, his moral pulls the reader in opposite directions. On the one hand, Montaigne claimed that "the rule of rules, and the universal law of laws, [is] that each man should observe those of the place he is in" (E I: 23, 86). On the other hand, he recognized that the variety and variability of custom allows us to reflect on the ordinance of our own laws and customs. When we do, we come to see that they are utterly without foundation.

Montaigne's interpreters have seen in this skeptical strategy oppo-site dangers. His reform-minded critics believe it produces a wooden adherence to the status quo. The orthodox and faithful accuse him of a dangerous relativism, which undermined the truth of traditional val-ues. In this respect, Michel Foucault's critics resemble Montaigne's. Foucault is alternately accused of anarchy and conservatism. Both charges issue, I think, from failure to appreciate the degree to which his work on institutions and modern power, like Montaigne's *Essays*, departs from more familiar forms of political writing. Political theoriz-ing, either explicitly or implicitly, seeks to organize social and political life as a whole. Montaigne and Foucault oppose the possibility of total organization, whether on the basis of fundamental political principles, human reason, or utopian ideals. In opposing a total conceptualiza-tion of our political situation, they must also oppose the possibility of its total reform. Because the public world is suspect – masks and appearances for Montaigne and regimes of power for Foucault – what reform is possible has to do with one's self and its relation to social and political realities, a reform that begins with the realization of the groundlessness of current values and institutions and thus, the realiza-tion that things can be otherwise. Both distrust the public sphere, and Foucault, similar to Montaigne, is faced with the challenge of articu-lating a politics without seeking to ground it in considerations of truth and freedom. John Rajchman, in his book on Foucault, remarks that "Foucault doesn't ask us to hope for a complete better form of life, but to imagine a time so different as to make our own time seem arbitrary."[18] And as William Connolly has correctly noted, it is Foucault's rhetorical devices that achieve the desired effect. Connolly writes, "[Foucault's] rhetorical figures, to use a phrase of Nietzsche's, incite us to '*listen* to a different claim' rather than to accept the find-ings of an argument: and they proceed this way because genealogy of the will to truth cannot present itself as a set of truth claims."[19]

The political implication of skepticism is that social and political change must be piecemeal and particular. From the point of view of political theorizing, skepticism's particularist politics is judged to be

---

[18] John Rajchman, *Michel Foucault: The Freedom of Philosophy* (New York: Columbia University Press, 1985).

[19] William E. Connolly, "Taylor, Foucault, and Otherness," *Political Theory*, vol. 13, 1985, p. 368.

either insubstantial and conservative or anarchistic. But from the point of view of skepticism, such a politics is consistent with the fragmented, transitory, and contingent nature of the public world. The example of Montaigne suggests why Foucault's critics, operating within a traditional conception of political discourse and its relation to political reality, beg the question against him in charging that his discourse undermines its own desire to critique modern power. Similarly, it begs the question against Montaigne to criticize him for conservatism or to attack him as a dangerous relativist.

Montaigne's aim, similar to Foucault's, was neither conservative nor reformist. But unlike Foucault, his was a politics that sought to enable both loyalty to and the possibility of criticism of customary laws. He wrote:

> Whoever wants to get rid of this violent prejudice of custom will find many things accepted with undoubting resolution, which have no support but in the hoary beard and the wrinkles of the usage that goes with them; but when this mask is torn off, and he refers things to truth and reason, *he will feel his judgment as it were all upset, and nevertheless restored to a much surer status.* (E I: 23, 84–5, emphasis added)

Where once customary values claimed the authority of truth, they are now seen as matters of choice and commitment. We live in accordance with them because it is useful to do so, but we do so without prejudice and dogmatism. What the reader of the *Essays* comes to see is the possibility of an attitude of deep doubt, but in its doubt the customary value is restored to a surer status of our own making. Starobinski strikes the right tone of appreciating this enabling aspect of skepticism.

> [A]quiescence in the inherited order is based, for the enlightened mind, on the infinite variety of usages and customs, among which no criterion of superiority enables one to choose: no criterion, that is, except for that of public tranquility and the survival of the community....
> [T]he convention to which the war-weary skeptical mind rallies is unlike the convention it earlier denounced: it is the same appearance but henceforth deprived of the foundation it once claimed, and which guaranteed it a timeless, not to say transcendental, authority.... What is finally recognized is the *usage* (the living moral order) that *appears* to best serve the general welfare. A loyalism becomes possible.[20]

[20] *Montaigne in Motion*, pp. 252–3.

It is one thing to suggest that Montaigne wants private doubt and public loyalty to coexist, making both constancy and criticism possible. It is quite another, however, to be persuaded of the coherence of their coexistence. Merleau-Ponty attempts to do so by noticing that skepticism is two-sided. On his reading of Montaigne, skepticism "means that nothing is true, but it also means that nothing is false. It rejects *all* opinion and *all* behavior as absurd, but it thereby deprives us of the means of rejecting any one as false."[21] Merleau-Ponty concludes from this that Montaigne's skepticism reinstates the truth of custom, albeit in a new way.

Though I am in sympathy with the tone of Merleau-Ponty's reading, I am not persuaded by this as an argument. The Pyrrhonian strategy indicates that there is no general argument for the coherence of doubt and conviction, conservatism and critique. Skeptical political discourse must remain dubious of attempts to mobilize arguments and to organize the appearances, ambiguities, and contingencies of the public in terms of theory. For its discourse to be more than merely doubt – for the politics of skepticism to have political content – it must eschew political assertions and oppose political theorizing without, at the same time, undermining possibilities for political activity. The political implications of the various rhetorical strategies of Montaigne's *Essays* are instructive. Unlike political theorists, Montaigne does not offer political principles or utopian ideals to guide political action nor does he assert a political agenda. Insofar as his skepticism reveals the groundlessness of our customary values and institutions, its goal is to open up possibilities for change and thus for political activity. Insofar as it seeks to oppose dogmatism and reduce violence, it fosters stability and order. Through proper attention to private life we can live with the tension between the two.

[21] Maurice Merleau-Ponty, "Reading Montaigne," in *Sign*, Richard C. McCleary, trans. (Evanston, IL: Northwestern University Press, 1964), p. 198.

5

Individuality and Common Goods

> When the inhabitant of a democratic country compares himself indi-
> vidually with all those about him, he feels with pride that he is equal of
> any one of them; but when he comes to survey the totality of his fellows
> and to place himself in contrast with so huge a body, he is instantly over-
> whelmed by the sense of his own insignificance and weakness. The same
> equality that renders him independent of each of his fellow citizens,
> taken severally, exposes him alone and unprotected from the influence
> of the greater number.[1]
>
> Alexis de Tocqueville, *Democracy in America*

Rousseau was our best diagnostician of the tension in social life
between our desire to be self-determining and our need for others –
what Kant would later call our "unsocial sociability." Rousseau's *First
and Second Discourses* remain among the most acute diagnoses of this
tension, and his *Social Contract* gives the best expression of the dilemma
for social theory created by it: "[how to] find a form of association that
defends and protects the person and goods of each associate with all
the common force, and by means of which each one, uniting with
all, nevertheless obeys only himself and remains as free as before."[2]
Rousseau's formulation suggests a way of thinking about democratic

---

[1] Alexis de Tocqueville, *Democracy in America*, vol. 2, (New York: Vintage Books, 1990),
   p. 10.
[2] Jean-Jacques Rousseau, *On The Social Contract,* Judith R. Masters, trans. (New York:
   St. Martin's Press, 1978), p. 53.

citizenship that is neither a form of liberal individualism nor its communitarian counterimage of citizenship constituted by antecedently given civic virtues. That, at least, is what I shall argue.

I suggested in Chapters 2 and 3 that individuality in the way Socrates represented it is essential for understanding democratic citizenship. It joins the capacity to call into question and resist the tyranny, dogmatism, and the leveling tendencies of mass culture with the capacity for self-examination. The capacity of self-examination is necessary not simply for determining how to live the best life; it is a necessary condition for democratic deliberation that requires citizens to be able to question their deepest convictions in light of the deliberative process. The deliberative approach to democratic participation offers an alternative to both liberal and communitarian formulations of democratic citizenship. From the deliberative perspective, liberalism undervalues the contribution the deliberative process plays in shaping an individual's interests. Communitarianism overestimates the presence of background consensus about civic virtues in democratic decision making, at least in the context of a pluralistic democracy, and, therefore, also underestimates the role of deliberation in creating common values. Neither view adequately appreciates the nature of individuality in a democracy.

Individuality – the capacity of self-examination as well as self-determination – is essential for democratic deliberation. Individualism, however, is a different matter. Individualism has come to stand, in the minds of many social critics, for all that is problematic about democracy, at least the liberal form that has characterized democracy today (for the most part). As we saw in Chapter 1, it is individualism that has been identified as the source of cynicism and democracy's discontent. Individualism has come to be associated with self-absorption, detachment, and indifference to others and to any sense of common goods. In what follows, I will seek to distinguish individuality from individualism and to argue for a conception of individuality that is conditioned, at least in part, by society and collective interests. And I will claim that democratic deliberation requires this conception of citizenship. My argument will arise out of an interpretation of Rousseau.

There are, of course, other paths than Rousseau's that one could take to the same end. George Kateb, for example, has marked his out through Emerson, Thoreau, and Whitman. In the essays that form the core of Kateb's argument for what he calls "democratic individuality," he returns to their rich formulations of that peculiarly American form of self-reliance and he seeks to show how their sense of democracy – of "the people" – counteracts the self-involved tendencies of individualism. "The meaning of the theory of democratic individuality," Kateb claims, "is that each moral idea [democracy and individuality] needs the other, both to bring out its most brilliant potentialities and to avoid the most sinister ones. A good tension would mark the relationship between these mutually dependent and mutually refining ideas."[3] Kateb quotes from Whitman's *Democratic Vistas*: "For to democracy, the leveler, the unyielding principle of the average, is surely join'd another principle, equally unyielding, closely tracking the first, indispensable to it, opposite.... This second principle is individuality."[4]

I think that careful attention to how Rousseau attempted to differentiate the leveling tendency of individualism from individuality and how he attempted to accommodate the tension between the individual and society will help to show why the tension is integral to democratic citizenship. Rousseau's theory of the social contract is meant to show how the individual becomes part of the social whole and at the same time remains a free and self-determining individual. On Rousseau's account, the social contract is supposed to produce "the total alienation of each associate with all his rights to the whole community" (SC, 53). Through the terms of the contract, each gives over his or her person to the general will, becoming thereby a part of the social whole. Because, according to Rousseau, this contract is between equals and is common to all, one becomes a part of the social body while obeying no other than one's own will. By giving each of ourselves to all, we relinquish our natural freedom but receive liberty in exchange. Through the contract we become part of the social whole yet are as self-determining as before.

Practically no one thinks this achieved a successful solution to the social dilemma that Rousseau had been so sensitive in exploring. The

[3] George Kateb, *The Inner Ocean: Individualism and Democratic Culture* (Ithaca, NY: Cornell University Press, 1992), p.79.
[4] Walt Whitman, *Democratic Vistas* (1871), in *Leaves of Grass and Selected Prose*, John Kouwenhoven, ed. (New York: Modern Library, 1950), 485.

most-offending passage in Rousseau that seems to threaten any possibility of solution – the one that has raised such serious problems
for interpretation as well as for political conscience – comes in the
Social Contract where he claimed that the social contract could remain
effective only if "whoever refuses to obey the general will shall be constrained to do so by the entire body, which means only that *he will be
forced to be free.*" I interrupt quoting the passage at this point momen-
tarily because it is on the emphasized phrase that Rousseau's critics
fix.[5] The claim that one can be forced to be free is as disturbing as
it is paradoxical. It has encouraged more than a few interpreters to
characterize Rousseau's position as a "totalitarian democracy," and
to dismiss Rousseau out of hand. This is the next sentence of the
passage: "For this is the condition that, by giving each citizen to the
homeland, guarantees him against all personal dependence" (SC, 55).
I will want this sentence to carry the interpretive weight. How can
giving ourselves to the homeland guarantee freedom from personal
dependence?

There have been three general lines of criticism of Rousseau that
argue that if this is the solution to the tension between individual and
society, the cure is worse than the disease. According to one line, there
is simply an irresolvable inconsistency between his ideal freedom –
as developed in the earlier *Discourse on the Origin and Foundations of
Inequality* – and his view of the general will that can force one to be free.[6]
Given this inconsistency, the critics claim, Rousseau's social contract
cannot produce both individual freedom and the subordination of
individual interests to the common good. The very terms in which the
problem is posed prevent its solution.[7]

According to a second, related line of criticism, Rousseau simply
fails to provide a plausible moral psychology that could account for
why individuals would voluntarily give up their natural condition and

---

[5] See, for example, J. L. Talmon, *The Origins of Totalitarian Democracy* (New York: Praeger
Books, 1960).

[6] This was the more common criticism of Rousseau offered by his contemporaries.
Recent commentators, while not agreeing with Rousseau's own claim for the unity
of his work, are less prone to charge inconsistency, seeing instead a developmental
coherence from the earlier to the mature views.

[7] See, for example, Richard Fralin, *Rousseau and Representation* (New York: Columbia
University Press, 1978), p.78f. Fralin contends that Rousseau recognized this and
moderated his expression of the problem later in the *Social Contract.*

contract with others to become subordinate to the general will.[8] According to a third line of criticism, Rousseau's solution to the problem he stated is thought to be no more than a conjurer's trick: That is, the only sense in which one could both give oneself to all and remain free is that one freely accepts one's own subordination.[9]

I want to reconsider Rousseau's solution to the social dilemma against the background of these criticisms. But to do so, I think it is useful to begin by recasting Rousseau's problem in terms of two strands of current social theory, each of which grows out of a criticism of liberal individualism. Understanding how Rousseau might respond to his critics, as interesting as it might be in its own right for historians of philosophy, is relevant for recent discussion. So I want to go to Rousseau with our issues in mind and then return to our issues on the basis of Rousseau.

The first criticism of liberal individualism grows out of critiques of modern social institutions such as those offered by Hannah Arendt and Michel Foucault.[10] The second is at the center of the debate between liberal political theorists and communitarians such as Michael Sandel and Charles Taylor.[11] I want to show how Rousseau's way of structuring a genuine social bond is consistent with self-determination, and even requires it. This will suggest why the way this debate between liberalism and communitarianism is currently cast is unhelpful. And it will suggest a conception of the democratic personality and citizenship required by democratic deliberation.

Critics of modernity such as Arendt and Foucault have claimed, though in different ways, that in its attempt to secure individual freedom, the modern age actually has resulted in the emergence of social institutions that increasingly intervene in, administer, regulate, normalize, and discipline every aspect of individual life. Their criticisms

---

[8] See, for example, Patrick Riley, *Will and Political Legitimacy* (Cambridge, MA: Harvard University Press, 1982).

[9] This is the sort of criticism suggested by Isaiah Berlin's discussion of Rousseau in "Two Concepts of Liberty" in *Four Essays on Liberty* (Cambridge: Oxford University Press, 1969).

[10] Hannah Arendt, *The Human Condition* (Chicago: The University of Chicago Press, 1958) and Michel Foucault, *Discipline and Punish* (New York: Vintage Books, 1979).

[11] Michael J. Sandel, *Liberalism and the Limits of Justice* (Cambridge: Cambridge University Press, 1982) and Charles Taylor, *Philosophical Papers 2: Philosophy and the Human Sciences* (Cambridge: Cambridge University Press, 1985).

suggest the need either to defend individual autonomy against the normalizing nature of modern society or to rethink society in a way that is compatible with individuality.

Communitarian critics of liberalism have argued against liberalism along contrary lines. They have claimed that a liberal conception of society, which is developed on the basis of the voluntary association of autonomous individuals, cannot provide the strong sense of a common good that is necessary for sustaining their social vision. According to this line of criticism, liberal social virtues, such as justice and equality, must reduce to individual interests. The result of liberalism is that community can amount to no more than an instrumental arrangement for mutual benefit. In contrast to the conception of individuals and society central to classical liberalism, communitarians urge a conception of the individual that is, at least partly, constituted by community and the common good – a conception in which belonging to one's community forms one's self-understanding as a citizen.

Brought together, these contrary strands of criticism allow us to recast Rousseau's problem. There is a fundamental tension between a conception of society that emphasizes the priority of autonomous individuals and a conception that gives prior claim to the common meanings and values of the community within which individuals think and act. On the former conception, the individual serves as the philosophical trump against the tendency of society to reduce diversity to conformity. On the latter, the priority of community serves to prevent social virtues from decomposing into merely individual interests. In coming to terms with the tension between autonomy and the requirements of community, it is necessary to resist the temptation to ease the tension in one direction or the other. On the face of it, neither direction seems promising. Attempting to resolve it in one direction detaches individuals so much from the surrounding values of their traditions and community that it becomes doubtful – in just the way that communitarian critics have suggested – how such detachment can yield a moral psychology for social virtues. If it cannot, then justice or equity can be no more than optional individual preferences. Attempting to resolve it in the other direction so radically situates individuals in their communities that it not only becomes doubtful how individuals can be distinct from the already given values that constitute them, it is doubtful how individuals so constituted could avoid uncritical acquiescence in those values. In terms of this tension, the problem is whether it is possible to have both individuality and a nonindividualistic sense of communal or social values. Rousseau's challenge is how to understand ourselves in relation to society in such a way that the common good forms part of our self-understanding at the same time that society makes possible individuality and a plurality of visions for one's life that individualism requires. My thesis is that Rousseau's solution to the problem suggests the possibility of assuring individuality within the context of irreducibly common social values that communitarianism requires; and furthermore, that this sense of individuality is integral to citizenship in a deliberative democracy.

There are three strategies for approaching Rousseau that I need to make explicit. First, whereas commentators sometimes separate Rousseau's earlier views in the *First and Second Discourses* from his later views in the *Social Contract* to sidestep problems of consistency, Rousseau always claimed that there was a unity to his entire work. While he may turn out to be wrong in his self-assessment, I will assume a unity unless the interpretive price becomes too great. Second, even Rousseau's more generous readers dismiss the first of the discourses, the *Discourse on the Sciences and Arts,* as merely an occasional piece designed more to earn his reputation than to engage in serious or convincing argument.[12] I intend, however, to bring it to the interpretive center to suggest how the criticisms of modern culture presented in it shaped his view of natural freedom, on the one hand, and placed constraints on the solution to the social dilemma offered in the *Social Contract,* on the other. Third, because at least part of the motivation for reconsidering Rousseau is the way his problem is posed in recent discussion, I will draw from that discussion certain distinctions and lines of analysis that might illuminate Rousseau's view in contemporary terms.

Rousseau's *Discourse on the Sciences and Arts* established his reputation as a "man of letters." It was written in response to an Academy of Dijon essay competition on the question "Has the progress of the sciences and arts done more to corrupt morals or improve them?" Remembering that this question was asked at the height of Enlightenment

---

[12] I discussed the *First Discourse* and its critics in ch. 3 of my *Philosophy in Question: Essays on a Pyrrhonian Theme* (Chicago: University of Chicago Press, 1988).

enthusiasm for the belief that the spread of scientific reason throughout society would produce freedom and social equality, Rousseau's
essay advanced the surprising thesis that "our souls have been corrupted in proportion to the advancement of our sciences and arts
toward perfection."[13] Though Rousseau won the prize and secured
his reputation with the discourse, he later judged it "the most fee-
bly argued" of his works[14] and commentators have generally shared
this view. Robert Wokler has written, for example, that he "find[s] it
difficult to disagree with Rousseau's own assessment of the text. Its
rhetorical flourishes may well have merited the prize for which it was
composed, but it seems to me much the least elegant, least consistent,
least profound, and – despite the fuss that it stirred – least original of
all his celebrated writings."[15]

In spite of the judgment of Rousseau and his commentators, the
theme of the essay – the role of the sciences, letters, and arts in cor-
rupting the individual and society – is one he returned to and elabo-
rated on several other occasions. It is the subject of his preface added
to his play, *Narcisse,* for example, and his *Letter to M. d'Alembert on
the Theatre.*[16] It is also a presupposition of his philosophy of education in *Emile.*[17] The arguments supporting this theme are deceptively
simple. They are presented in a summary passage early in the *First
Discourse.*

[T]he sciences, letters, and arts.... spread garlands of flowers over the iron
chains with which men are burdened, stifle in them the sense of their original
liberty for which they seemed to be born, made them love their slavery, and
turn them into what is called civilized peoples. Need raised thrones; and the
sciences and the arts have strengthened them.... civilized peoples cultivate

[13] Jean-Jacques Rousseau, *The First and Second Discourses,* Roger D. and Judith R. Masters,
trans. (New York: St. Martin's Press, 1964), p. 39.
[14] Jean-Jacques Rousseau, *The Confessions,* J. M. Cohen, trans. (Baltimore: Penguin
Books, 1954), p. 329.
[15] Robert Wokler, "The 'Discours sur les sciences et les arts' and Its Offspring: Rousseau
in Reply to His Critics," in *Reappraisals of Rousseau* (New York: Barnes and Nobel
Books, 1980), p. 251.
[16] Jean-Jacques Rousseau, "A Preface to 'Narcisse: or the Lover of Himself,'" Benjamin
R. Barber and Janis Forman, trans., *Political Theory,* vol. 6, 1978 and "Letter to
M. d'Alembert on the Theatre," in *Politics and the Arts,* Allan Bloom, trans. (New
York: Cornell University Press, 1968).
[17] Jean-Jacques Rousseau, *Emile, or On Education,* Allan Bloom, trans. (New York: Basic
Books, 1979).

talents: happy slaves, you owe to them that delicate and refined taste on which you pride yourselves; that softness of character and urbanity of custom . . . in a word, the semblance of all the virtues without the possession of any. (D, 36)

There are four connected but distinguishable claims being made in this passage that are developed in this and the other essays. First, under the guise of virtue, the sciences, letters, and arts foster relations of need and dependency that are the antitheses of freedom. Second, by identifying the virtues with those accidental capacities and talents some individuals have for cultivating the sciences, letters, and arts, they introduce a "disastrous inequality into society" (D, 58). Third, relations between people in modern culture, being based on dependency and distinctions of talent, produce "double men" who appear to act for others but act always only for themselves (E, 41). Fourth, a consequence of the dissolution of virtue produced by the advancement of the sciences, letters, and arts is the corruption of taste, where civilized peoples all seem to be stamped in the same mold and become "this herd called society" (D, 38).

Taken together, the first and second claims imply the project of the *Discourse on the Origin and Foundations of Inequality*. Because social relations based on need and dependency are the corruption of virtue, natural freedom will be understood by negating those features of culture that produce our dependence on others. The general point of Rousseau's argument was that talents and abilities are merely contingent and accidental features of individuals. Not only can they not give rise to moral worthiness, they are the source of political inequality. In the *First Discourse* Rousseau had asked: "What brings about all these abuses if not the disastrous inequality introduced among men by the distinction of talents and the debasement of virtues?" (D, 68). And he had argued that because what is taken for merit in modern society derives from the views others have of a person's worthiness, considerations of merit *enslave* us through the opinions of others. This claim about merit forms part of the fourth criticism: Progress in the sciences, letters, and arts produces "this herd called society." I will turn to a fuller discussion of this criticism shortly. For now it is useful to state that it turns on the way concern for the opinions of others fosters a corrupted form of self-regard that produces conformity to the opinions others have of us.

By contrast to the accidental distinctions of merit valued by modern society, genuine virtue must arise out of what is original and essential to the individual prior to learning and culture. Freedom must be found in one's own sense of one's worthiness. The agenda for the *Second Discourse* is set by the arguments of the first: The model for self-sufficient wholeness will be discovered in what is essential to the self apart from social relations and the opinions of others.

In the *Second Discourse*, Rousseau distinguished natural or physical inequality from moral or political inequality. The former results from differences in health, strength, qualities of mind and the like; the latter from "[those] different privileges that some men enjoy to the prejudice of others, such as to be richer, more honored, more powerful than they or even to make themselves obeyed by them" (D, 101). The purpose of the *Second Discourse* was to show how the latter sort of inequality originated out of a form of social organization that placed primary value on the former. Rousseau's device for tracing the progress of moral inequality was, of course, the hypothesis of the state of nature that "strip[ped] this being, so constituted, of all the supernatural gifts he could have received and of all the artificial faculties he could have acquired by long progress – considering him, in a word, as he must have come from the hands of nature" (D, 105).

Of course, Hobbes had claimed that the state of nature was a state of war because human beings were motivated by self-interests. Rousseau claimed, however, that Hobbes had incorrectly attributed to individuals in their natural condition those characteristics that are a product of society. "[Hobbes] ought to have said that since the state of nature is that in which care of our self-preservation is the least prejudicial to the self-preservation of others, that state was constantly the best suited to peace and the most appropriate for the human race" (D, 129). It is tempting to think that the reason Rousseau was able to paint a different picture of the state of nature than Hobbes was that he attributed not only an instinct for self-preservation but also a sense of pity to natural man. Though the instinct of pity will be essential for his account of a sense of common humanity, it is not the presence of pity in the natural state that makes it the least prejudicial to the self-preservation of others.

Ironically, the reason the natural state is best suited to peace is that in that state, one is so stripped of needs and reason as not only to not require others but not even to be aware of others. This is how Rousseau summed up such a condition:

Let us conclude that wandering in the forest, without industry, without speech, without domicile, without war and without liaisons, with no need of his fellow-men, likewise with no desire to harm them, perhaps never even recognizing anyone individually, savage man, subject to few passions and self-sufficient, had only the sentiments and intellect suited to that state; he felt only his true needs, saw only what he believed he had an interest to see; and his intelligence made no more progress than his vanity. (D, 137)

Rousseau later wrote in *Emile* that "[n]atural man is entirely for himself. He is numerical unity, the absolute whole which is relative only to itself or its kind" (E, 39). He called this natural form of internal unity and self-sufficiency *amour de soi* to distinguish it from that corrupted form of self-interestedness that arose from culture. It is clear from the passage of the *Second Discourse*, however, that in conceiving of our natural condition as one of minimal needs, devoid of reason and oblivious of others, *amour de soi* is not so much an achievement as self-sufficiency gained by default. Natural freedom is a condition of self-sufficient unity only because it is defined in the absence of awareness of others. It is also defined in the absence of a conflict between original instincts and the intellect that emerges only in response to growing needs. When needs grow, intellect comes to replace original instinct, and one must take notice of others and come to depend on them. One begins to measure one's self in terms of them. When one person acquires power over another, distinctions based on the natural inequalities and talents come to be valued. *Amour de soi* is replaced by *amour propre* – natural self-love becomes a corrupted form of self-regard that desires distinction and singularity rather than self-sufficiency.[18]

Because we must take notice of others and come to depend on them, what I have called self-sufficiency by default is, of course, not possible for us. Nevertheless *amour de soi* in the state of nature suggests that freedom and individuality within society will involve a form of self-regard or self-valuing that is independent of our concern with how others view us. The task for Rousseau's social theory is to reconstruct

[18] See Nicholas Dent, "Rousseau and Respect for Others," in *Justifying Toleration: Conceptual and Historical Perspectives*, Susan Mendua, ed. (Cambridge: Cambridge University Press, 1988), pp. 115–35.

society in a way that depends upon and reinforces *amour de soi*. The first stage in this reconstruction is his positing of a natural instinct of pity.

According to Rousseau's moral psychology, once one begins to measure one's self against others, the sentiment of pity – the natural feeling toward others in the face of their suffering – serves to prevent that notice of others from being purely self-interested. Thus it prevents *amour de soi* from becoming merely *amour propre*. In the *Second Discourse* Rousseau had described this nonreflective natural sentiment of pity this way; "moderating in each individual the activity of love of oneself, [it] contributes to the mutual preservation of the entire species . . . [which inspires us with this maxim of natural goodness]: *Do what is good for you with the least possible harm to others*" (D, 133). The role pity comes to play for Rousseau was made clearest in the education of Emile. There, Rousseau wrote:

It is man's weakness which makes him sociable; it is our common miseries which turn our hearts to humanity. . . . Every attachment is a sign of insufficiency. If each of us had no need of others, he would hardly think of uniting himself with them. Thus from our very infirmity is born our frail happiness. A truly happy being is a solitary being. God alone enjoys an absolute happiness. . . . It follows from this that we are attached to our fellows less by sentiments of their pleasures than by the sentiment of their pains. . . . If our common needs unite us by interest, our common miseries unite us by affection. (E, 221)

Need binds us to others because of our own interest in self-preservation. It leads us to compare ourselves with others, producing envy or vanity. Pity in the face of the suffering of others puts us in the place of others. By imagining their misery it carries us out of ourselves. Without a natural instinct of pity or compassion to draw us to others as such, the social contract could be no more than an association for mutual benefit. But this is precisely the account of contract theory Rousseau referred to disparagingly as a "social knot" and that he claimed produced "double men" who appear to act out of the interest of others while acting only for themselves.

There is, however, an interpretive problem about the relation between pity and *amour de soi* that cannot be minimized. Because natural self-love is understood in terms of a self-sufficient wholeness – a self that lacks division and is not dependent because it takes no notice of others – it seems implausible that pity could be an original sentiment of an undivided self.[19] If both self-love and pity are original instincts, then it seems that natural freedom cannot be characterized as a lack of division within the self. However, if the sentiment of pity is absent in the state of nature, Rousseau would lack an adequate moral psychology to explain the transition from the state of nature through the purely private interests typical of *amour propre* to the creation of a society of public persons. How are we to deal with this problem? It is necessary to speak for Rousseau in a way that preserves self-dependent wholeness as the ideal of freedom yet motivates the creation of society as he understood it.

This inconsistency can be addressed, I think, by exploring the implications of the hypothetical character of the state of nature. It is standard to realize that most social philosophers who begin with the state of nature are not offering it as a historical thesis. In the preface to the *Second Discourse*, Rousseau had made clear to the reader that the state of nature he imagined was "a state which no longer exists, which perhaps never existed, which probably never will exist" (D, 93). I think, however, that for Rousseau we must realize that he not only does not suppose that anyone ever actually lived in a condition of natural freedom, it seems clear that no one ever could. Because our natures are divided – divided between ourselves and others as well as divided within ourselves between instinct and intellect – natural freedom is not really possible. The state of nature presents an ideal of freedom achieved by negating those features of contemporary society that lead to a corrupted individual. Yet because we are moved by instincts of self-preservation as well as pity, we realize that an undivided self-sufficiency has not existed and would not exist even if it were possible to return to a natural condition. It is for that reason that society properly formed is necessary for resolving the natural conflict that exists between self-preservation and a feeling for the suffering of others, between instinct and intellect, and between our desire for independence and our need of others. The fact that one is divided within one's self and in relation to others lends all the more weight to the necessity of a social contract. Through it we

---

[19] For a careful discussion of this inconsistency see John Charvet, "Rousseau and the Ideal of Community," *History of Political Thought*, vol. 1, 1980, pp. 69–80.

reclaim freedom comparable to what was imagined by abstraction in the natural state.

Already, then, it is possible to suggest against one line of criticism how Rousseau's work forms a consistent whole. In the *First and Second Discourse*, the *Social Contract*, and the education of *Emile*, Rousseau offered a narrative of an ideal wholeness, the emergence of a division within the self and from others, the corruption and dissolution of virtue through culture, and a proposal for how virtue might be recast and reclaimed through the social contract, and by educating individuals for autonomy and for citizenship.

The criticisms in the *First Discourse*, and this abstract conception of self-dependent unity of the self that is opened up, implies an initial constraint for the solution to the problem of the *Social Contract*. Freedom achieved through the social contract will be different from natural freedom in that it must be achieved through others. Yet it will be equivalent because in relations with others, one's sense of worthiness will arise from one's self and one will obey only one's own will. Because it is the conflict between self-interested individuals that produces the corruption of virtue and social duty that Rousseau diagnosed in the *First Discourse*, the social contract must achieve reconciliation through a form of association that is not based on self-interestedness.

This constraint on the solution to the problem of the *Social Contract* needs to be filled out. Rousseau claims that social relations grounded in mutual self-interestedness are merely the appearance of social union. Though he makes this claim in the *First Discourse*, a fuller expression is given to it in the preface to *Narcisse*. There, he wrote:

[O]f all the truths I offer here to the consideration of wise men, this one is the most astonishing and the most cruel. Our writers like to regard absolutely everything as 'the political masterpiece of the century': the sciences, the arts, luxury, commerce, laws – and all other bonds which, in tightening the social knot with the force of personal interest, make men mutually dependent, give them reciprocal needs and common interests, and require that all pursue the happiness of others in order to be able to pursue their own.[20]

The thrust of his criticism is that society, conceived of as an association of self-interested individuals for mutual benefit, is true neither to our

[20] "A Preface to 'Narcisse'," p. 549.

natural disposition of self-love nor to social duty. The point to consider is what this criticism implies for a genuine social union and thus what it implies for his solution to the problem of finding a form of association in which we enter society but remain as free as before.

First, if an association of self-interested individuals for mutual benefit constitutes a social knot, then a social bond can be achieved only out of a form of recognition of others that does not arise from our need for and dependence on them – a form of recognition that is not decomposable into individual self-interest.[21] This is the point of Rousseau's distinction between "the will of all" and "the general will." The former is merely the sum of individual wills. The latter is a collective will that is *irreducibly* collective. I shall return to this point shortly. Second, because relations of need and dependence create a knot rather than a bond, a genuine social contract with others must be such that giving one's self to all is consistent both with self-determination and association. The contrast between the view of social relations that Rousseau criticizes and the view of association he commends can be illuminated by recent discussion of different senses of community.

In *A Theory of Justice,* John Rawls distinguishes a conception of community modeled on the ideal of private society in which relations with others are purely instrumental for realizing mutual advantage from a sense of community in which human beings "share final ends and value their common institutions and activities as good in themselves" (ATJ, 522). What motivates the distinction for Rawls is the desire for a nontrivial sense of human sociability and social union. To that end he argues that his notion of "justice as fairness" provides that sense of community. Just institutions are a shared end and are thought to be an intrinsic good by all members of the social union. My intent is not to explore Rawls's view but to distinguish his view of social union from a third notion of community suggested by Michael Sandel in his criticism of Rawls. Sandel calls Rawls's view of social union a sentimental conception of community. It involves both self-interested and cooperative feelings toward others. Sandel contrasts the sentimental and the

---

[21] This way of formulating the issue was suggested by Charles Taylor, "Irreducibly Social Goods," in *Philosophical Arguments*, Cambridge, MA: Harvard University Press, 1995, pp. 127–45 and by John R. Searle's "Collective Intentionally," presented at the Oberlin Philosophy Colloquium, March 1988.

instrumental conception that Rawls distinguishes with a constitutive conception of community.

Whereas the instrumental and sentimental senses of community differ from each other in terms of the quality of motive that produces social union, they are alike in that they conceive of community as a voluntary union of originally asocial individuals. By contrast, the constitutive sense of community involves a form of self-awareness in which "community would describe not just a *feeling* but a mode of self-understanding partly constitutive of the agent's identity" (LLJ, 150). In developing this contrast, political theorists, such as Sandel and Charles Taylor, claim that the individualistic conception of social union cannot provide the sufficiently rich account of community necessary to support a strong sense of commitment to the common good. On the individualistic account, communitarian sentiments, such as justice, are reducible to merely individual preferences. Sandel puts the contrast this way:

[T]o ask whether a particular society is a community is not simply to ask whether a large number of its members happen to have among their various desires the desire to associate with others or to promote communitarian aims – although this may be one feature of a community – but whether the society is itself a society of a certain kind, ordered in a certain way, such that community describes its basic structure and not merely the dispositions of persons within the structure. For a society to be a community in this strong sense, community must be constitutive of the shared self-understanding of the participants and embodied in the institutional arrangements, not simply an attribute of certain of the participants" plans of life (LLJ, 173).

The space of the debate between liberal political philosophers and communitarian critics such as Sandel is drawn between individualistic and constitutive accounts. These are not only alternative but also apparently incompatible.

How might Rousseau's view of a genuine social bond be placed in terms of this recent debate? It is clear from his criticisms in the *First Discourse* and the preface to *Narcisse* that he, similar to Rawls, rejected an instrumental conception of community. He rejects it in the first place because it is a form of association that is merely the appearance of a social union. Second, it assumes self-interestedness as the only motivation for the social contract. It seems, then, that because the social contract is a voluntary association motivated by natural

sentiments of self-love as well as pity, the resulting social union will
be similar to Rawls's sentimental conception. It is clear from the *Social
Contract* that the voluntary act of association *transforms* the private self.
It produces a public person with a will that is general – that is, it results
in a form of association in which contracting parties understand themselves in terms of an irreducibly general will. The result of Rousseau's
contract, then, is something like Sandel's constitutive notion of community because as parts of a public person, individuals are constituted
by a common good that cannot be decomposed. What Rousseau seems
to provide is an individualistic account of the origin of social relations –
what is referred to in recent discussion as "methodological individualism" – with a socially constituted account of the individuals that result
because they are constituted by their relation to the general will.

If this individualistic account of the origin of social union is consistent with a constitutive conception of individuals who are formed by
that union, this suggests that perhaps the terms in which the debate
between liberals and communitarians is sometime cast need to be questioned. I will return to this suggestion at the end, but for now, the point
I wish to draw from this way of casting Rousseau's position has to do
with the way the social contract makes legitimate the loss of natural
freedom and solves the social dilemma.

The purpose of social contract theories is to provide justification for
government through the consent of individuals. There are, however,
three distinct ways the social contract can be thought to convey justification to the governmental institutions it produces.[22] First, because
the contract is entered into voluntarily by autonomous individuals,
autonomy could be thought to make legitimate whatever is the outcome of the contract. This is apparently what Hobbes thought justified
the exchange of freedom for security even if the cost of security was an
absolute tyrant. Second, the contract could convey legitimacy through
the recognition of equal interests in self-preservation of the contracting parties and the reciprocal benefits resulting from association. This
is the sort of contract suggested by Rawls when individuals choose in
the original position and where the veil of ignorance assures equality

---

[22] Two of these distinctions were suggested by Sandel's discussion of contract theory,
though they do not coincide with his account. See *Liberalism and the Limits of Justice*,
p. 106–7.

of interests and reciprocity. It is also the way Rousseau is often interpreted.[23]

This cannot be exactly right for Rousseau, however. What it would
justify is at best the will of all rather than the general will. At worst it
results in the paradoxical view that the sovereignty of the general will
is justified because through it one realizes one's private good. The
latter result would produce what Sandel has called the sentimental
conception of community in which recognition of the common good
becomes simply one of an individual's interests. Reciprocity, however,
is inadequate to account for the kind of transformation of the private
self and natural freedom that Rousseau thought the social contract
produced: "[I]n place of the private person of each contracting party,
this act of association produces a moral and collective body, composed
of as many members as there are voices in the assembly, which receives
from this same act its unity, its common *self*, its life, and its will" (SC, 53).

There must be a third sense of justification, one in which individuals
recognize equality as an irreducibly communal value. Equality in this
sense is a necessary condition for entering the contract. It is a form
of recognition and contract that must be presupposed in accounting
for the transformation of the private will into a public will. I shall
refer to this form of recognition as *mutuality* rather than reciprocity.
By mutuality I mean a form of collective intentionality possessed by,
but not reducible to, individual agents and resting on a sense of
communal awareness of others as participants of essentially cooperative activity. The contrast between mutuality and reciprocity is roughly
the one that Amy Gutmann has drawn between liberal egalitarianism
and what she calls communal or radical egalitarianism. Gutmann's distinction is drawn on the basis of her analysis of Rawls, and though it is
beyond my purpose to enter that discussion, the way she sums up her
analysis is instructive for interpreting Rousseau.

---

[23] This is the sort of interpretation suggested by Joshua Cohen in "Reflections on
Rousseau: Autonomy and Democracy," *Philosophy and Public Affairs* 15 (1986) and
by John Plamenatz, "On le forcera d'être libre," in *Hobbes and Rousseau: A Collection
of Critical Essays*, Maurice Cranston and Richard S. Peters, eds. (New York: Anchor
Books, 1972). Plamenatz writes, for example, that "man formed by society, who reasons and is a moralizer, is *egalitarian:* he prefers himself to others and yet is dependent on them, and it is therefore his interest to be recognized by them as an equal,"
p. 329.

[L]iberal egalitarianism is too individualistic because it reduces the value of equality to individual interest. Equality is a value for a community taken as a whole, rather than a means of satisfying the interests of individuals within that community taken separately. A less radical translation of this criticism, however, might be the following: Because people must be non-individualistic if they are to enter into [Rawls's] original position, the reasoning from self-interest within the original position can be more accurately viewed as reasoning from a *moral* interest in community that each of us as real, particular individuals has outside the original position.[24]

In these terms, the social contract conveys legitimacy to the general will not simply because it is a voluntary arrangement or even because each contracting party has an equal interest in self-preservation that social arrangements will foster. It is legitimate because it is entered into by individuals who recognize themselves and are recognized by others as mutually participating in collective activity. In this sense, Rousseau's position is more closely connected to what is today called *deliberative democracy*. Deliberative democrats are critical of both liberal and communitarian models of democracy.[25] Both theories misunderstand the role of deliberation in democratic consensus formation. On the liberal view, individuals come to the deliberative process or vote for their representatives to the deliberative process with already formed interests, and consensus formation is the process by which those interests are brokered and aggregated. Communitarians assume that individual interests are constituted by antecedent communally held beliefs about the common good and that democratic decision making takes place within the framework of shared understanding about the common good. For deliberative democrats, the liberal conception implies that individual interests are left unchanged by the processes of deliberation. They underestimate and undervalue the role deliberation should have in shaping individual interests through collective activities. Communitarians overestimate the role of shared values in the democratic process, especially in an essentially pluralistic culture. They

[24] Amy Gutmann, *Liberal Equality* (Cambridge: Cambridge University Press, 1980), p. 221.
[25] See Jurgen Habermas, "Three Normative Models of Democracy," in *Democracy and Difference: Contesting the Boundaries of the Political*, Seyla Benhabib, ed. (Princeton: Princeton University Press, 1996), pp. 21–30 and John S. Dryzek, *Deliberative Democracy and Beyond: Liberals, Critics, Contestations* (Oxford: Oxford University Press, 2000), ch. 1.

underestimate how deliberation can contribute to shared values among diverse citizens. Deliberative democrats begin where liberals do, by assuming that in a pluralistic democracy, differences about values are both real and persistent. But they conceive of democratic deliberation as a process through which individuals across different perspectives of values, gender, race, and economic condition, come together to fashion consensus about collective interests. That process presupposes a willingness on the part of citizens – even an expectation – that one's interests will be transformed by the deliberative activity. Common goods are not merely the aggregate of private interests, nor are they antecedently discovered through the democratic process. They are fashioned through the deliberation. In this sense, what conveys legitimacy to the outcome of democratic decision making is not the vote of the majority, but the legitimacy of the process by which the vote was arrived at. This is the process and the sense of equal participation that can make legitimate a general, that is, irreducibly social will.

To see why this is so and how it is related to pity or compassion as an original instinct, consider how Rousseau concludes Book One of the *Social Contract*. "I shall end this chapter and this book with a comment that ought to serve as the basis of the whole social system. It is that rather than destroying natural equality, the fundamental compact on the contrary substitutes a moral and legitimate equality for whatever physical inequality nature may have placed between men, and that although they may be unequal in force or in genius, they all become equal through convention and by right" (SC, 58). Recall that Rousseau had criticized his contemporaries who had identified moral progress with progress in the sciences and arts. They had erected virtue on distinctions based on talents and abilities that culture valued, virtues that one had by by luck. The result is that they exacerbated natural inequalities. These distinctions in talent and ability, which are the source of envy and vanity, are traced back to a corrupted form of self-love in which we measure ourselves against others. However pity, unlike envy or vanity, takes us outside of ourselves. Through pity we imagine the suffering of others, moderating the tendency self-love has of becoming *amour propre*. This gives rise to our sentiment of common humanity. The sentiment of common humanity that pity provides is necessary for entering the social contract. It provides the psychological basis for the mutuality of recognition suggested by Gutmann's account of communal equality. Without it one could not enter into an association with others and remain as free as before.

The plausibility of this suggestion rests on showing why a familiar objection to Rousseau is misdirected. It has been argued that the very terms in which he expressed our social dilemma – how to find a form of association in which uniting with all others a person remains as free as before – renders the solution impossible. When conflicts arise between individual interest and the general will, why, if one is as free as before, would one choose to obey the general will. Or if one chooses to obey the general will, in what sense is one truly as free as before.

I do not wish to minimize the paradoxical nature of Rousseau's claim that whoever refuses to obey the general will can be forced to be free. I do not think, however, that it undermines his view of freedom. The way the criticism is sometimes made suggests that the transformation from natural freedom to conventional or political freedom is simply the shift from self-determination in the absence of social constraints to self-determination under law. What this misses, however, is the fundamental difference between a private will and the public will and the significance of the difference between civil and moral freedom. On the first issue, it must be stressed that it is not just that by way of the social contract that the *object* of a private will becomes general. If that is what it comes to, then the transformation of private to public will would be no more than the inclusion of the general good as one of an individual's interests. Rather the will becomes general through the recognition that civil freedom is possible only when each contracting party wills the good of all. The opposite of civil freedom on Rousseau's account would be subjugation to a superior will. This condition can exist, however, only when private individuals force their wills on others. Thus it can only exist when the contract has become void. So long as the contract remains, the general will is one's own will and among contracting parties there is no superior.

But Rousseau distinguishes civil freedom and its conditions of possibility from moral freedom. "To the foregoing acquisitions of the civil state could be added moral freedom, which alone makes man truly the master of himself. For the impulse of appetite alone is slavery, and obedience to the law one has prescribed for oneself is freedom" (SC, 56). Whereas civil freedom has to do with one's relations with others, moral freedom has to do with one's relation to one's self. Moral freedom is the achievement within society of *amour de soi* and its opposite is not subjugation by a superior will but *amour propre*. John Plamenatz is surely right in claiming that it is with regard to moral freedom that Rousseau asserts that man can be forced to be free. The purpose of this paradoxical claim is to draw attention to the social and psychological conditions of moral freedom.[26] The sentence following the assertion that one can be forced to be free is that "this is the condition that, by giving each citizen to the homeland, guarantees him against all personal dependence" (SC, 55). It is only by conforming to the general will *that is one's own* that natural freedom in relation to one's self can be regained as moral freedom within society. To be governed by *amour propre* and private interests is to remain enslaved by appetite and the opinions of others no matter how much civil freedom one may enjoy. But to conform to the general will that one agreed to when entering the contract is not only to acquire civil freedom through mutuality with others, one's sense of worth can be determined by and is dependent on one's self.

There is a final constraint that Rousseau's criticisms of progress in the sciences, arts, and letters in the *First Discourse* places on the solution to the social dilemma formulated in the *Social Contract*. It connected the idea of conformity to the general will. The least-developed criticism, but the one that most resonates with contemporary critiques of modernity, is that the dissolution of virtue produced by the requirements of civilized culture *levels out individuality*. He formulated the criticism in the following way:

Today, when subtler researches and a more refined taste have reduced the art of pleasing to set rules, a base and deceptive uniformity prevails in our customs, and all minds seem to have been cast in the same mold. Incessantly politeness requires, propriety demands; incessantly usage is followed, never one's own inclinations. One no longer dares to appear as he is; and in this perpetual constraint, the men who form this herd called society, placed in the same circumstances, will all do the same things.... (D, 37–8)

Later in the *First Discourse* Rousseau asked what an artist would do when confronted with a culture that had reduced taste to the art of pleasing: "He will lower his genius to the level of his time" (D, 53).

[26] Plamenatz, "On le forcera d'être libre," p. 324.

Rousseau's argument depends on the psychology of *amour propre*. *Amour propre* is a regard for one's self that arises from comparisons between one's self and others. The person motivated by *amour propre* seeks to achieve prestige and distinction, but just because *amour propre* is a sense of self-worth and distinction sought in relation to others, it depends on the opinions others have of us. Instead of achieving uniqueness or individuality, then, the person motivated by *amour propre* is enslaved by the opinions of others – molded by and leveled to their opinions.[27]

I do not pretend that one can find in this complaint anything similar to the dark and persuasive analysis of the normalizing effects of modern society that one finds in Hannah Arendt's *The Human Condition* or Michel Foucault's *Discipline and Punish*, nor do I think that there is any interpretive gain in suggesting that Rousseau anticipated postmodernist criticism. The point I wish to draw from his criticism is this: if modern culture produces a pernicious uniformity in which individuals are enslaved by the opinions of others and reduced to the level of their age, then it will be a condition for the solution of the social dilemma that in a true social contract individuality, both as self-dependency and diversity, will be possible. It cannot be the enforced homogeneity thought by some critics to follow from the absolutism of the general will. Nor can individuality be the self-interested drive for singularity of *amour propre*. More strongly, it must follow for Rousseau that only within that form of association that this version of the contract produces can genuine individuality be possible, because it is only then that *amour de soi* can be reclaimed.

Because this last claim seems *prima facie* incompatible with the absolute sovereignty of the general will as well as with the constitutive notion of community, it is necessary to elaborate this requirement. Rousseau's work suggests two different ways of coming to understanding what individuality is. One derives from his account of the state of nature. The other and less obvious is in terms of Rousseau's own position in relation to the culture that he criticized. It is not necessary to say much about the first because what I have already suggested about natural freedom applies to individuality understood in terms of it. Though

---

[27] See Dent, "Rousseau and a Respect for Others," pp. 118–19 for an illuminating discussion of this point.

natural freedom suggests an ideal of individuality as a self-dependent unity, it is individuality by default as it is had not in relation to others but in their absence. More does need to be said regarding the second suggestion.

In few other philosophers was there such an intimate connection between the inner life of the author and the substance of his thought. Not only did he exploit the relation between autobiography and philosophy in *The Confessions, Jean-Jacques Judge of Rousseau,* and *The Reveries of a Solitary Walker,* he was acutely conscious of his own position at the margins of his culture. That marginality constituted the fulcrum for his criticism of it.[28] What he had written of Molière's misanthrope in the *Letter to d'Alembert on the Theatre* could be said equally of himself: "[W]ho then is the misanthrope of Molière: A good man who defeats the morale of his age and the viciousness of his contemporaries; who, precisely because he loves his fellow creatures, hates in them the evils they do to one another."[29]

Understood in terms of his criticism of culture in the *First Discourse* or in terms of the character of Rousseau, it would seem that individuality is achieved by renouncing one's culture and refusing to lower one's self to the level of one's age.[30] However, individuality of the state of nature is asocial and had by default, and the individuality of the marginalized social critic is merely antisocial. Neither can offer the prototype of individuality that is supposed to be achieved through the social contract. Together, however, they suggest what social individuality might be. First, it is a self-determining unity. Unlike what is represented in the *Second Discourse,* however, it is constituted in relation to others through the general will. Second, it requires that what is marginal with respect to mass society becomes integral to social union, allowing genuine diversity to be possible. That is, when private individuals unite and become public persons it cannot produce "this herd called society." In this sense, the solution to the social dilemma cannot

---

[28] See Bronislaw Baczko, "Rousseau and Social Marginality," *Daedalus,* vol. 107, 1978.

[29] "Letter to d'Alembert," p. 37.

[30] In an especially illuminating anthropological and historical study of individualism, Louis Dumont has suggested something similar in contrasting what he calls the *outworldly* individual who is self-sufficient by renouncing the world with the *inworldly* individual of modern individualism. Louis Dumont, *Essays on Individualism: Modern Ideology in Anthropological Perspective* (Chicago: The University of Chicago Press, 1986).

just be the conjurer's trick of being free only because one chooses one's own suppression. Instead, the conditions of the contract guarantee the reintegration of the self through association with others. In this way *amour de soi* or moral freedom or individuality becomes possible.

What inclines interpreters to think that individuality is incompatible with the sovereignty of the general will is both the fact that Rousseau's account of direct democracy was based on the model of small and homogeneous societies, and the result that, because the general will is the expression of consensus about the common good, individuals must conform themselves to the social consensus. With regard to this last point, interpreters draw attention to Rousseau's claim about being forced to be free, which I have already discussed, but it bears repeating that the general will is not an alien will to which I submit. It is the will I and others make through the deliberative process and, thus, it becomes my will. But does the requirement of consensus seem to militate against the possibility of real individuality?

The assumption behind this criticism is that diversity, originality, and, thus, individuality can be assured only on the basis of a political conception of freedom as noninterference. It suggests that only through noninterference, compatible with a like freedom for all, can we have sufficient control over ourselves to determine our lives in our own way.[31] This purely negative conception of liberty – the conception of John Stuart Mill, at least in *On Liberty* – supposes that the only sort of freedom deserving of the name is the freedom to pursue one's own interests in one's own way. Yet the claim that one can be forced to be free implies a more substantive, positive conception of liberty. The conflict between Rousseau and these critics can be expressed as the conflict between negative liberty and this more substantive concept.[32] Rousseau's conception of original freedom shares with the friends of negative liberty the idea that freedom is self-determination that comes from an independence from others. But in claiming that the solution to the social dilemma can be found only through a form of association

---

[31] This is the force of Berlin's argument against positive liberty in "Two Concepts of Liberty."

[32] See Berlin's "Two Concepts of Liberty" and Charles Taylor, "What's Wrong with Negative Liberty?" in *Philosophical Papers 2: Philosophy and the Human Sciences*, for unusually careful discussions of the distinction between negative and positive conceptions of liberty.

in which *amour de soi* is possible, he is committed to a positive conception for two reasons: first because moral freedom is a matter of achieving an authentic sense of self-regard; and second, because authentic
self-regard cannot be guaranteed merely by social relations of noninterference. I cannot settle the debate for and against positive liberty.
I merely want to suggest that positive liberty is not simply compatible with individuality, it is a necessary condition for it. It constrains any
solution to the social dilemma because it is the absence of individuality
that Rousseau deplored in his criticism of French society.

Finally, to return to the contemporary expression of the social
dilemma that Rousseau had addressed. I want to suggest briefly
how reconsidering Rousseau might cast light on the current debate
between liberalism and communitarianism, and the criticism that
modern society invades and administers every aspect of individual life.
The problem posed for contemporary social theory is how to reconcile plurality or diversity among individuals with a nonindividualistic
commitment to common goods. The terms in which the problem is
often formulated, however, seems to force one to choose between individualistic or constitutive accounts of community. The result of posing
the problem this way is that the emphasis on individualism leads to the
conclusion that common goods are simple among the interests of individuals within society. By contrast the emphasis on community leads to
the threat of homogeneity and acquiescence in the prevailing social
values. The assumption is that individualistic and constitutive accounts
of community and the conceptions of the self proper to them are
mutually exclusive, but they also seem to yield unacceptable choices
either way. The lesson to be learned from Rousseau, however, is that
the line along which the contemporary debate is structured is badly
drawn.

If we take the continuity of Rousseau's thought between the *First and
Second Discourses* and the *Social Contract* then we can come to see that the
"solution" to the dilemma of the individual and others is to hold in tension individuality and the common good. His sense of individuality –
both self-dependent and singular – resists the capacity culture has to
level individuals to the prevailing values. His sense of the common
good prevents individuality from becoming a corrupted form of self-
love. In Whitman's terms – quoted earlier – "the unyielding principle
of the average, is surely join'd another principle, equally unyielding,

closely tracking the first, indispensable to it, opposite. . . . This second principle is individuality."

Philosophers sometimes fall prey to the conceit that interpreting other philosophers is the same as interpreting the world. It is one thing to reposition Rousseau against his interpreters or to position him in relation to contemporary philosophers. It is another thing to say how we might think and act differently as a result. The authors of *Habits of the Heart* observed that "finding oneself means, among other things, finding the story or narrative in terms of which one's life makes sense."[33] For most of us the tension between our sense of ourselves and our sense of responsibility to others is very real. It is real because we live with deep skepticism about the capacity of public discourse to rise above competing special interests, because we are ambivalent about commercialized culture that simultaneously fosters selfishness and conformity, and because we are skeptical about the capacity of democratic institutions to foster both diversity and common social values. The tension between individuality and the common good was very real for Rousseau too. I think his narrative can help us see how we might, and how we must, maintain the tension in productive ways. He helps us see how we must remain distrustful in the face of the capacity of culture and claims for the common good to smother individuality, and therefore why we must stay vigilant; and at the same time we must remain cautious, and therefore skeptical, about excessive claims of self-reliance. The capacity to maintain a productive tension between the demands of self and the demands of society is what characterizes the democratic individuality – citizens who deliberate with others about common interests and in accepting deliberative consensus remain as free as before.

---

[33] *Habits of the Heart*, p. 81.

6

Democratic Education

When citizens rule in a democracy, they determine, among other things, how future citizens will be educated. Democratic education is therefore a political as well as an educational ideal.[1]

Amy Gutmann, *Democratic Education*

A university can be to a political philosopher what a good laboratory is to a biologist. This is even more the case if one happens to be an academic administrator as well. I have had the privilege of being both. I have spent thirty-five years of my life in universities studying and teaching philosophy and for fifteen of those years I also have served in administrative roles. Through the interactions between my philosophical interests and administrative responsibilities I have come to appreciate the challenges of education in a democracy as well as education's democratic possibilities.

Philosophers from Plato to Dewey have recognized that education is political theory in practice. For better or worse, the state and education are joined. Plato understood that to achieve the ideal Republic he had to control the content of the education of philosopher kings and kick Homer out of the curriculum. Political revolutionaries

[1] Amy Gutmann, *Democratic Education* (Princeton: Princeton University Press, 1987), p. 3. Subsequent references are to "DE" and page number in the text.

and reformers have always known this. Controlling education is only marginally second to capturing the offices of the press and controlling the airwaves for revolutionary success. So what better place for a politically minded philosopher to be than a provost's office? There are obvious advantages to this vantage point for both the philosopher and the administrator. After observing university politics for a while, it is easier to appreciate Rousseau's claim that Hobbes mistook the state of nature for the nature of society, especially a society that cultivates the arts and sciences. Observing the academic left and the academic right duking it out over the great books and the canon, it is easier to appreciate the dynamics of culture wars where lives are at stake, not just reputations and self-respect. On the positive side, it has allowed me to appreciate the fact that universities are in one sense distinctive and in another typical of institutions in American life. They are typical in the characteristics they share with other nongovernmental institutions – economic impact or social and political influence, for example – that make them useful case studies for the role of institutions in democratic culture more generally. They are distinctive because education has been so intertwined with democracy, historically through the needs of citizenship and more recently with aspirations for access and mobility. Perhaps more than any other public institutions, universities have faced and responded to the challenges of democratic culture, especially of an increasingly diverse culture. Though very much still a work in progress, universities have met head-on our nation's history of racism and ethnic and gender discrimination, not only through affirmative action admissions policies but by transforming curricula and scholarship. The changes have been hard fought both within and outside of the academy, and again, universities are still works in progress in this regard. But there are few other institutions where meeting the challenge of race in America's history and its culture have become so much a part of its self-understanding. It has been within universities that the many subtle and not so subtle ways that women were discouraged in the classroom, thwarted in their aspirations, and blocked in their careers were confronted, transforming scholarship, curriculum, and the rights and rituals of the academy in the process. It has been within universities that the divisions of class, privilege, and economic means have been confronted through "need blind" admission policies, affirmative action initiatives, financial assistance strategies, and academic support programs to expand access to higher education and the social and economic mobility it makes possible. Universities have been at the crossroads and often in the crosshairs of some of the deepest issues of our pluralistic democratic culture. One cannot be engaged in these issues without thinking seriously about liberty and its limits, about social justice and equal opportunity, and about the nature of democracy.

The relationship between universities and the course of American democracy has been complex. The complexity is both historical and conceptual. Historically, one of the originating ideals of the new democracy was that education, including higher education, was important to its success. In 1779, in the earliest days of the democratic revolution, Thomas Jefferson submitted a bill to the Virginia legislature that, if it had passed, would have provided a system of education from primary school through university at public expense. His "Bill for the More General Diffusion of Knowledge," included a selection system through which young men of ability could rise through the system to university education regardless of family background and means.[2] Jefferson was not successful in this attempt and it was years later when he was able to achieve part of his vision with the founding of the University of Virginia. But Jefferson's ideas were influential and he was not alone in his commitment to public education. Other signers of the Declaration of Independence – John Adams, Benjamin Franklin, and Benjamin Rush, to name the three most prominent – also proposed systems of education at public expense in their states. Why should education be so important to the new democracy that it should be provided at taxpayer expense?

Jefferson was the most articulate in giving an answer. At various times, he offered three interconnected rationales. The first grew out of his essentially Enlightenment sensibility, honed in part by his reading of the French *philosophes*. Ignorance enslaved the mind and only education could liberate people from the powers of tyrants and the superstitions of priests. In a letter to George Wythe, written from Paris in

---

[2] A convenient source for this and other key documents about Jefferson's views on education is the appendix of James B. Conant, *Thomas Jefferson and the Development of American Public Education* (Berkeley: University of California Press, 1962).

1786, Jefferson justified his commitment to public education this way:

> I think by far the most important bill in our whole code is that for the diffusion of knowledge among the people. No other sure foundation can be devised for the preservation of freedom, and happiness. If any body thinks Kings, nobles, or priests are good conservators of the public happiness, send them here. It is the best school in the universe to cure them of that folly. They will see here with their own eyes that these descriptions of men are an abandoned confederacy against the happiness of the mass of people. The omnipotence of their effect cannot be better proved than in this country particularly, where notwithstanding the finest soil upon earth, the finest climate under heaven, and a people of the most benevolent, the most gay, and amiable character of which the human form is susceptible, where such a people I say, surrounded by so many blessings from nature, are yet loaded with misery by kings, nobles and priests, and by them alone.[3]

But Jefferson brought to Enlightenment liberalism a democratic sensibility. Publicly supported education would break down the artificial, inherited aristocracy that was characteristic of Europe and would replace it with an aristocracy of merit. In an exchange of letters with John Adams, Jefferson reflected back on his failed attempt to get legislative approval for publicly financed education. This is the rationale he gives to Adams in retrospect:

> At the first session of our legislature after the Declaration of Independence, we passed a law abolishing entails. And this was followed by one abolishing the privilege of Primogeniture, and dividing lands of intestates equally among all their children, or representatives. These laws, drawn by myself, laid the axe to the root of Pseudo-aristocracy. And had another which I prepared been adopted by the legislature, our work would have been compleat. It was a Bill for the more general diffusion of learning. This proposed to divide every country into wards of 5 or 6 miles square, like your townships; to establish in each ward a free school for reading, writing and common arithmetic; to provide for annual selection of the best subjects from these schools who might receive at public expense a higher degree of education at a district school; and from these district schools to select a certain number of the most promising subjects to be completed at an University where all useful sciences would be taught. Worth and genius would thus have been sought out from every condition of life, and compleately prepared by education for defeating the competition of wealth and birth for public trusts.[4]

---

3 "Letter to George Wythe, from Paris, August 13, 1786," in Conant, p. 99.
4 "A Letter to John Adams from Monticello, October 28, 1783," in Conant, p. 109.

But finally, Jefferson also well knew the risks inherent when the people rule. While he was on the opposite side of Madison and the other Federalists, he was not naïve about the risks of democratic rule. Education was necessary if the people are to rule. It has been said that in a democracy one depends on the wisdom of strangers. It is, therefore, in our mutual interest to support the education, including higher education, of citizens in a democracy as our fate depends on them. This was a new and radical idea because it rested on a new and radical conception of citizenship.

In one way or another Jefferson's rationales have informed the shape of public policy about education, including higher education, for most of our history. This is not to say that they have not been added to and contested over time. But variations of the idea that in a democracy education is a public good have been an important rationale for the extraordinary public investments in universally available primary and secondary education, and for the creation of publicly supported colleges and universities. There have certainly been other rationales. With respect to higher education, for example, the first Morrill Act – signed into law by Lincoln in the midst of the Civil War that would decide whether America's experiment with democracy would continue – provided land grants to establish universities in each of the states to serve the need for agricultural and technical expertise in a nation set on westward expansion. The GI Bill was supported not only because it rewarded returning veterans of World War II for their service and sacrifice, but because it served the needs of the postwar economy. The National Defense Education Act of 1958 provided grants and loans for students in science and technical areas as part of national defense policy in the wake of Sputnik. The omnibus Higher Education Act of 1965, which authorized the most significant public investment in higher education to date, was part of "The Great Society" and was a centerpiece of its vision for combating racial and economic inequality by underwriting access to higher education regardless of need and race. The history of investment by the states in higher education is similar. Whether for citizenship, economic development, social justice, or national defense, for most of the history of the United States, higher education as been considered as much, perhaps more, a public good as a private value.

That idea, however, has been losing its hold on policy makers. For much of the twentieth century, higher education policy at the federal level and in the states supported expanded and affordable access to higher education. State budgets provided direct support to public universities and colleges to offset the cost of education for the sons and daughters of its citizens, and until the last decades of the twentieth century, states provided the lion's share of higher education funding. At the federal level, through a system of grants, loans, and work-study programs, students were supported to close the gap between parents' ability to cover costs and the actual cost of education. Affordable access to higher education was supported at substantial public expense because higher education was deemed a public good. But with the successive reauthorizations of the Higher Education Act of 1965, federal policy has sifted the balance of support for students with need from outright grants to low-interest loans, with the result that an increasing number of students are graduating with unconscionable personal debt. State support of public higher education has eroded – due in part to other, nondiscretionary budgetary pressures such as Medicare and prisons – to the point where in many cases it constitutes the smallest portion of a university's budget. As a consequence, the cost of attending public colleges and universities has shifted from states to students and their parents through escalating tuition and fees.

Whether through conscious policy making or not, the consequence of these shifts is that higher education is increasingly thought of as primarily a private good: as an individual benefit that individuals ought to be expected to pay for themselves. With this shift, the rationale for publicly supported higher education has tipped the public policy-making rationale for higher education in an exclusively economic direction. The standard argument that presidents and provosts of public universities and colleges make at their state houses is that higher education is as important for the state's economic development as good roads. It is part of the economic infrastructure. It is the argument that is made because it is the argument that matters for policy makers.

It is not unreasonable to think that because individuals reap benefits from higher education they should pay the costs. And, of course, this has been the case all along for the wealthy and for those who have been willing to pay for the advantages of expensive private institutions. And

certainly higher education has significant enough economic development implications to count those among the reasons that public
investment makes sense. But my worry is that we have lost sight of the
democratic purposes of higher education.

My interest in this chapter is with higher education, and primarily
with public higher education – both its distinctive democratic possibilities and how universities might serve as a model for the role of institutions in democratic life more generally. There are many ways in which
questions about the nature of democratic education apply equality to
all levels of education. Amy Gutmann, in her excellent book, *Democratic Education*, addresses many of the common issues and there is
little I disagree with and I have little to add to her thoughtful analysis.
But my experience and thinking has been about higher education and
I will confine my attention to that. And I am primarily interested in
public higher education because by virtue of being public, there is a
more direct relationship between the purposes of public universities
and the public trust. But the line between public and private higher
education is less sharp than it once was. Furthermore, private institutions are increasingly thinking about themselves in terms of their
public responsibilities and their place in a pluralistic, democratic culture. But the connection between public universities and colleges and
the needs of democracy are inescapable in ways that are less so for
private institutions. Finally, I will be using higher education, universities, and universities and colleges somewhat interchangeably. While
the distinction between universities and colleges is useful for certain
purposes, it is not a useful distinction for the broad and general issues
of democratic education I am interested in posing.

Higher education and American democracy have not only been
linked historically, they are linked conceptually, a linkage they share
with universities in the West more generally. Whether by conscious
design or not, universities serve both the processes of social reproduction – transmitting the values, traditions, and expectations of
society – and the processes of social criticism and transformation of
those very values, traditions, and expectations. This is an unusually difficult position to occupy – the line between social reproduction and
social criticism has been a shifting one, and the tightrope between is
unavoidably unstable. Many outside of the academy criticize universities and threaten their funding because they believe that universities

are much too engaged in criticizing society. Many within academia believe that universities have become so entangled with the interests of government and business or the prevailing ideology that they merely instantiate the culture, thus ceding their critical position. This view is gaining currency within academia especially as universities refashion themselves in response to eroding public financial support.[5] Universities are increasingly being run like corporations. The entrepreneurial professor is emerging as the ideal type. Students are talked about and coming to think of themselves as customers. The balance between liberal learning and professional education is increasingly tipping toward professional education. There seems to be a tectonic shift taking place that is producing what one group of authors have aptly referred to as the advent of "academic capitalism."[6]

Let me consider one such argument from within the academy. In *University in Ruins*, Bill Readings has argued that the universities in the West, and especially in the United States, have lost their way.[7] Readings's interest is with the idea of the modern university in the West and its decline. He takes the historical model for the modern university in the West to be the German university as envisioned by Wilhelm von Humboldt, founder of the University of Berlin. Humboldt's model embodied a specific view about the nature of the university in relation to the cultural identity of the nation-state. Readings summarizes the model this way:

The plan outlined by Humboldt for the University of Berlin synthesized the fundamental reorganization of the discourse on knowledge by which the University took on an indirect or cultural function for the state: that of the simultaneous search for its objective cultural meaning as a historical entity and the subjective moral training of its subjects as potential bearers of that identity. . . . Knowledge must be neither totally undetermined nor empirically determined in its application. Rather, it must be determined in reference to the indeterminate ideal of absolute knowledge. This ideal thus entirely

5 I am especially grateful to Kate Spillane for the opportunity to talk and think together about this during the course of her senior thesis, *University, Inc.*, University of New Hampshire, spring 2004.
6 Sheila Slaughter and Larry L. Leslie, eds. *Academic Capitalism: Politics, Policies, and the Entrepreneurial University* (Baltimore: The Johns Hopkins University, 1997).
7 Bill Readings, *The University in Ruins* (Cambridge, MA: Harvard University Press, 1999). Subsequent references are to "UR" and page number in the text.

restructures the medieval opposition between the active life and the contemplative life. . . . The University's social mission is not to be understood in terms of either thought or action. The University is not just a site for contemplation that is then to be transformed into action. The University, that is, is not simply an instrument of state policy; rather, the University must embody thought as action, as striving for an ideal. This is its bond with the state, for the state and the University are two sides of a single coin. The University seeks to embody thought as action toward an ideal; the state must seek to realize action as thought, the idea of the nation. The state protects the action of the University; the University safeguards the thought of the state. And each strives to realize the idea of national culture. (UR, 68–9)

Readings is right that this has been an influential model and that an important way of understanding the idea of the university is the relationship among the university, the nation-state, and the idea of national cultural identity. While he gives a rather sophisticated interpretation of the relationship and its demise in the wake of globalization and postmodern (he prefers the term *posthistorical*) culture, his story line is fairly straightforward. With globalization and the decline of the nation-state, the idea of cultural identity can no longer provide the *raison d'être* for the university. Without the ideal of culture as its rationale, the humanities can no longer occupy the central role in the university's self-understanding. The ideal of the professor and the role of the university in producing liberally educated citizens are no longer sustainable. A new type, the administrator, emerges and becomes the central figure in the university. Readings glosses Jacques Barzun's view in *The American University: How it Runs, Where It Is Going*, where Barzun proposes the creation of nonacademic but enlightened administrators. Readings concludes that "the central figure of the University is no longer the professor who is both scholar and teacher but the provost to whom both these apparatchiks [administrators] and the professors are answerable" (UR, 8). I must admit that I like that. But Readings doesn't. On his account, provosts, enamored with the corporation, seek to replace the organizing rationale of national cultural identity with the pursuit of excellence. But the result is that students become consumers, and "the contemporary University busily transforms itself from an ideological arm of the state into a bureaucratically organized and relatively autonomous consumer-oriented corporation" (UR, 11). But that is not the worst of it. Because the idea of excellence is vapid and vacuous, the idea of the university can no longer sustain itself. The university is in ruins.

In the face of the university in ruins, Readings sees only three possibilities for the posthistorical university.

> Either we can seek to defend and restore the social mission of the University by simply reaffirming a national cultural identity that has manifestly lost its purchase (the conservative position), or we attempt to reinvent cultural identity so as to adapt it to changing circumstances (the multicultural position). A third option is to abandon the notion that the social mission of the University is ineluctably linked to the project of realizing a national cultural identity, which is tantamount to ceasing to think the social articulation of research and teaching in terms of a *mission.* (UR, 90)

Readings pursues the third option. He argues that the posthistorical university should abandon its nostalgia for culture and recognize that it is an unlikely model for combining the Enlightenment ideal of a rational community with an appreciation for multiculturalism. On this last point Readings says, "Anyone who has spent any time at all in a University knows that it is not a model community, that few communities are more petty and vicious than University faculties (suburban 'model communities' might be an exceptions). And yet the story persists. The University is supposed to be the potential model for free and rational discussion" (UR, 80). Instead, he proposes that

> we should recognize that the loss of the University's cultural function opens up a space in which it is possible to think the notion of community otherwise, without recourse to notions of unity, consensus, and communication. At this point, the University becomes no longer a model of the ideal society but rather a place where the possibility of such models can be thought – practically thought, rather than thought under ideal conditions. (UR, 20)

There is a great deal that is deeply insightful about Readings's analysis of the modern idea of the university. And a great deal of what he says about the state of the humanities, corporatization of higher education, and universities in search of a reason would resonate with anyone who has spent much time in universities lately. I think, however, that Readings misses the mark about universities, in the United States at least, even though some of his analysis are illuminating and even though I have sympathy for aspects of what he thinks universities ought to be about. Why he misses the mark is connected with why I think his second option is still viable for American universities, though not in exactly the form in which it has often been articulated. Readings is not wrong in thinking that there is an identity crisis in higher education today in the United States and elsewhere. But his diagnosis and, as a result, the particular way he shapes the alternative possibilities for the university misses the mark.

I am suspicious of four tendencies in his analysis. The first is the idea of the university. It seems to me that it makes as much sense to conclude from Readings's analysis that this essentially nineteenth-century conceit – "The Idea of the University" – has outlived its usefulness as that universities have lost their reason to be. This seems especially – perhaps always – the case with American universities. There are over 3,500 postsecondary institutions in the United States. Of those, while many are public, most are private. Most students by far are educated in public institutions. Of the privates, some are based on religion, some of those based on religion are in name only, and some are secular. Some publics and privates are historically black, most are historically white. Most private colleges and universities are nonprofit, but some are profit making and the largest of these is publicly traded on the stock exchange. There are research universities, liberal arts colleges, urban institutions, residential colleges, and commuter colleges, some which just enroll undergraduates, others are for advanced study only, and so on. Within this array, there are a number of exemplary types, and while the dynamics of mission envy is tending to settle universities and colleges around a smaller number of these types, there is still sufficient diversity that we should be cautious about the "Idea of the American University." And to avoid appearing to contradict myself later, I do not intend to suggest what "The Democratic Idea of the University" is or should be. Rather, I want to make the more modest suggestion that despite the diversity of models and missions, we need universities and colleges to be agents for democracy.

Readings's second tendency that worries me is that he thinks that the window into the soul of the university today is what presidents and provosts say about universities. Having been a university administrator, it pains me to say that this is merely one window and not always the best. The administration of universities is only one of many windows for looking into the university. This is the case for the obvious reason that universities are many things. Debates over the curriculum offer another window – and not just debates among humanities professors. The changing nature of the professoriate is another. The relationship between universities and their communities is another. And so on. One does not necessarily see the same thing from each of these vantage points and whether or not that is a bad thing is debatable.

While universities and colleges are primarily about education – about the production and transmission of knowledge – that is not all they are about. In many ways universities and colleges *are* businesses. Consider the following: Universities, and even small colleges, are often among the largest employers in their areas. In addition to professors, they manage housing and food services. They maintain buildings and grounds and motor pools. Some own clinics and hospitals. They require payroll offices, mail services, and housekeepers. They are often the largest landholders in their area. They are often the largest consumers of water and energy resources and among the largest producers of waste. Public universities hold the largest percentage of state-owned buildings in most states. Universities and colleges are located in areas of rural poverty, in blighted city neighborhoods, and in suburban enclaves of wealth and privilege. Some universities are turning city neighborhoods and rural areas into enclaves of wealth and privilege – through research parks, alumni villages, gentrification of housing, and commercial investment. These are legitimate material for thinking about the place of universities and colleges in communities, states, and the life of a democratic nation.

Readings's third tendency is to think that the current condition of some humanities disciplines in universities is equivalent to the condition of universities. Strangely, this conceit is shared by humanities professors and by social conservatives such as William Bennett.[8] They both overestimate the role of controversies over the great books in the 1980s and 1990s in the self-understanding of colleges and universities. Social conservatives overestimated its impact on students because they underestimated the abilities of students to sift through the noise. Both Readings and the social conservatives draw the wrong conclusions from these debates. To be sure, they were marked by a good deal of incivility and ideological posturing and they forced a good deal of anxiety about

[8] See William J. Bennett, *The De-Valuing of America: The Fight for Our Culture and Our Children* (New York: Simon and Schuster, 1992).

the humanities: about their current condition and their place in the scheme of things. But the glass-half-full interpretation is that universities and colleges are and should be the places where the disciplines go through crises of faith from time to time. And the humanities have not been the only place in the university where this self-examination has taken place. The more important lesson of the so-called culture wars is that the curriculum matters enough to fight about. It matters not just for college catalogs and degree requirements. It matters because it expresses a philosophy of education of an institution, the collective view of faculty about what is important. That is worth fighting over. My regret is that the reason the fight is important was so rarely brought into the classroom and put to the service of students' education. This, it seems to me, was the sensible suggestion of Gerald Graff's book, *Beyond the Culture Wars*.[9] Make the controversies part of the education of our students.

Readings's fourth tendency is to think that what is wrong with universities today is just an instance of what is wrong with globalized – read that "Americanized" – capitalist culture generally. I can't resist quoting the hyperbolic way Readings makes this last point:

> Global "Americanization" today (unlike during the period of the Cold War, Korea, and Vietnam) does not mean American national predominance but the realization of the contentlessness of the American national idea, which shares the emptiness of the cash-nexus and of excellence. Despite the enormous energy in attempts to define "Americanness" in American Studies programs, one might read these efforts as nothing more than an attempt to mask the fundamental anxiety that it in some sense *means nothing* to be American, that "American culture" is becoming increasingly a structural oxymoron. (UR, 35–6)

I resist this interpretation not simply because I am a touchy American former provost and Readings was writing from Canada. I think it misunderstands something fundamental about American cultural identity. The history of the United States has, in an important sense, been a history of the contested nature of the idea of America; and its contested nature is an essential aspect of the idea. Political parties began in the United States because of fundamental disagreement

---

9 Gerald Graff, *Beyond the Culture Wars: How Teaching the Conflicts can Re-vitalize American Education* (New York: Norton Publishing, 1992).

about the meaning of the American Revolution, and they have continued through competing claims about who are the true custodians of the idea of American. Victories in the fight for social justice have come by contesting what and who is to constitute "We the People." It has been the subject of imaginative writing at least since Hawthorne's and Melville's novels and Whitman's poetry. Some of the richest of our cultural expressions is found in how successive waves of immigrants, including those who were forced here in slavery, and their offspring have struggled with what it is to be American. It is the struggle of an upper-middle-class black woman in Paule Marshall's *Praisesong for the Widow*,[10] and of Gogol in Jhumpa Lahiri's *Namesake*[11] and of Chang-Rae Lee's *Native Speaker*.[12] It is contested in Spike Lee films. Coltrane and Tupac have enlarged it as much as Aaron Copland and Charles Ives. It is even contested in kitchens and commentaries on American cuisine (another phrase that some would say was oxymoronic).

More than simply recoiling at Readings's claim about the vacuousness of American culture, I am dubious of those, like Readings, who drape Horkheimer's and Adorno's analysis of the culture industry and commodification over everything that moves in the late Enlightenment West, and especially in the United States. Not that theirs is not a powerful analysis for understand a great deal that is troubling in Western culture generally and in America. But I don't think that commodification of knowledge is the root of the problem of American universities. The vision of the professor as entrepreneur and the student as customer, while present and worrisome, is still peripheral. My own view is that what is wrong with corporatization of higher education is not that it turns knowledge into a commodity of exchange, but that its managerial ethos puts at risk the democratic possibilities inherent in the ways universities are governed, possibilities that are capable of resisting the commodification of education. Being undemocratic might be fine for corporations, but it is not fine for universities. What has been distinctive about American universities – and universities in the West generally – is our tradition of shared governance. This is also what drives business people and legislators wild. They believe the

---

[10] Paule Marshall, *Praisesong for the Widow* (New York: Putnam, 1983).
[11] Jhumpa Lahiri, *Namesake* (Houghton Mifflin, 2002).
[12] Chang-Rae Lee, *Native Speaker* (New York: Riverhead Books, 1995).

inmates are in charge of the prison. They can't believe that a man-
ager must seek the consent of workers. It sometimes drives university
administrators wild too, waiting years for the curriculum to be revised,
or dealing with the demands of student senates. But is has been central to the success of American universities and it is central to their
democratic possibilities.

One of the compelling aspects of the deliberative turn that democratic theorizing has taken is its aim to enlarge and deepen democratic possibilities beyond electoral politics and legislative processes.
Universities, as important democratic institutions, have been, and can
be again, places for democracy to flourish. I'm far less cynical than
Readings about this possibility. It requires, however, that we reassert
the importance of shared governance for the life of universities and
rethink it not as a contest among faculty, students, administrators, and
trustees but as deliberative, democratic consensus formation.

What are the democratic possibilities of universities and colleges?
There is much more to this question than how we should educate our
students, though this is a central aspect of the question. How we educate students for democratic citizenship is a fundamentally important
issue. It is just not the only issue. To think, as we faculty are prone to do,
that it is unseemly to believe that universities and colleges are about
more than teaching and research conceals other responsibilities we
have. For example: Who do universities hire and how are they compen-
sated? The living wage issue, brought to prominence by students and
workers at Harvard University, is an issue about the responsibilities of
universities and colleges, as influential nongovernmental institutions,
in a democratic society. The plight of itinerant faculty employed per
course without other benefits is an issue about the responsibilities of
universities and colleges in a democratic society, and so are the issues
of responsible stewardship of lands and scarce resources, the quality
of the workplace, and the responsibilities of universities and colleges
to their neighbors and in their communities.

This suggests that the question, "What is democratic education?" is
several questions. First, who can legitimately control what democratic
education is? Amy Gutmann has argued that a democratic theory of
education must involve, among things, "principles that, in the face of
our social disagreements, help us judge (a) who should have authority
to make decisions about education, and (b) what the moral boundaries
of that authority are" (DE, 11). We should expect that an answer to

the question "who should share authority" will have all the constitutive incompleteness and contestation as to who "We the People" are. The tradition of shared governance in universities – even though that tradition is eroding, especially in the ways that some corporate practices are introduced into universities – provides a basis for modeling how the boundaries of authority are drawn between interested stakeholders and those who can claim expertise in the disciplines, educational philosophy, and governance.

Second, what roles should universities, as influential institutions, play in democratic culture? At a minimum, they should be responsible stewards and good citizens. They share this responsibility with banks, churches, hospitals, philanthropic foundations, and so forth. And they can become models. Land grant universities were charted on the promise that university expertise would be extended to the needs and good of rural America, and the past few years have seen that promise renewed and reinvigorated for the information age.[13] Many cities have seen their inner-city campuses evolve into a new institutional type, the urban university, self-consciously defining themselves in terms of the needs of their cities.[14] Many private universities in cities that historically build walls around their campuses and their blighted neighbors have opened up to their neighbors as resources and have tackled some of the most daunting problems of inner cities. The University of Pennsylvania is an unusually good example. All of this is enormously encouraging. But doing good for the good of the community is not, of itself, democratic. Too often we overwhelm our neighbors by the sheer power we wield and by our habit of thinking we already know what they need. Universities and colleges need to be engaged with our neighbors and our communities as deliberative partners with all that implies about mutuality and respect and about the possibility it opens up that our views about the good will be shaped in the process.

And finally, how should we educate citizens for democracy? Here again, there is a good deal to be heartened about. Prominent higher education organizations such as the Association of American Colleges

---

[13] See the National Association of State University and Land Grant Colleges, Kellogg Commission reports, "Renewing the Covenant," http://www.nasulgc.org/Kellogg/.

[14] See, for example, the Great Cities Universities partnership, http://www.greatcitiesnet.org/.

and Universities have made democratic education the centerpiece of much of its programming.[15] Faculties in universities and colleges across the country have rethought curricula in response to the needs of more diverse students and considered enlarging scholarly perspectives that incorporate race, gender, and sexual identity. Responding to the call to renew civic life, universities and colleges have expanded opportunities for students to volunteer in their communities and service learning has become a powerful pedagogy for both learning and civic responsibility. As encouraging as all this is, it tends to reduce democratic education to multicultural curricula and civic responsibility. Important as this is, the view of democracy that I have been championing in this book suggests something more and somewhat different.

To see how, let me begin with the idea of democratic citizenship and civic responsibility that is implied in service learning pedagogy, something I strongly support. In a recent collection of essays on higher education and civic responsibility, the authors of one essay make an explicit connection between citizenship and service learning as an alternative way of thinking about citizenship. They distinguish three concepts of the democratic citizen:

1. Rights-bearing members of a representative political system who choose their leaders through elections. This "civics" view of citizenship stems from a view of democracy mainly as representative government and the rule of law.
2. Concerned members of communities who share common values and are responsible to each other for their community. This rendering of citizenship, defined by the "communitarian" philosophy, is also regularly associated with ideas of "civic society."
3. Public problem solvers and coproducers of public goods. This perspective is based on a work-centered philosophy of democracy that views authority for the commonwealth residing among the citizenry. It is associated historically with the political idiom of commonwealth in American history.[16]

---

[15] See http://www.aacu-edu.org/.
[16] Harry C. Boyte and Nancy N. Kari, "Renewing the Democratic Spirit in American Colleges: Higher Education as Public Work," in *Civic Responsibility and Higher Education*, Thomas Ehrlich, ed. (Phoenix, AZ: Oryx Press, 2000), p. 40.

It is the third conception of citizenship that they take as the promise for renewal of democracy – citizenship as public work – and this is what they believe is fostered through service learning. Students are engaged in their communities, addressing real needs and developing a sense of citizen responsibility to and for the commonwealth.

As commendable as this idea is, it does not seem to touch one of the deepest issues of our culture. It fosters the idea of the citizen as the responsible individual engaged in public work. While this is a meaningful counterweight to the culture of inwardness and narcissism, it does not convey or foster the sense of citizenship required in a culture where individuals must work together across the differences that constitute us a pluralist democracy to achieve agreement about our collective interests. It does not capture the relational aspect of democracy that the deliberative conception places at its center.

To see how, let me return to the paradox of democracy at the turn of the century that I sketched in the Introduction and use that as a way of framing some thoughts about educating students for democracy. I quoted economist Amartya Sen as saying the most important thing to occur in the twentieth century was "the emergence of democracy as the preeminently acceptable form of governance."[17] His view is widely held. Yet the idea of liberal democracy at home is deeply strained, especially when seen in the light of the strains of pluralistic democracy in America. Jean Bethke Elshtain's book *Democracy on Trial*[18] should serve to balance our optimism about democracy abroad. Her theme has run throughout this book. Democracy is in a particularly perilous condition in our country. Elshtain chronicles the ways in which we find ourselves being pulled between an increasingly fragmented society along the lines of race and gender, and nostalgia for the more homogeneous culture of an earlier day. Elshtain begins her account of democracy's perils with the ironic observation of John Courtney Murray that "disagreement is a very difficult thing to reach" (DT, xi). She believes that it is the task of a democratic disposition and democratic institutions to be able to reach disagreement, and she uses the task of reaching disagreement as a lever for diagnosing the fragile

---

[17] Amartya Sen, "Democracy as a Universal Value," *Journal of Democracy*, 10, 1999, p. 3.
[18] Jean Bethke Elshtain, *Democracy on Trial* (New York: Basic Books, 1995). Subsequent references are to "DT" and page number in the text.

condition of democracy and our need for a new social covenant. The "new social covenant," she writes, "is not a dream of unanimity or harmony, but the name given to the hope that we can draw on what we hold in common even as we disagree" (DT, 31).

This, it seems to me, is the best formulation of the challenge educators face in a pluralistic democracy. How are we to educate citizens and foster institutions that allow us to differ in ways appropriate to a pluralistic society, yet find the common ground necessary for social commitments and collective responsibilities? Optimism about the spread of democracy and Elshtain's distress about its fragility in our pluralistic culture provide a powerful framework for situating the cultural context of thinking about democratic education. This cultural context offers us the possibility to foster in our students an understanding of the hopes and risks of pluralistic democracy and, at a minimum, to give students occasions to reflect on this cultural context and to think about their own education in its terms.

The requirements of a pluralistic society have, of course, motivated a good deal of recent rethinking of the curriculum, most obvious in our attempts to deal directly with issues of race, ethnicity, and gender in the curriculum, and in requiring that students be introduced to non-Western cultural perspectives. But there are other, less obvious areas of the curriculum that also need to be rethought from needs of democratic society. Think for a moment about how we justify science in the general education curriculum. Why do we believe that it is important for students to study biology, for example? Not why biology students or premed students should study biology, but why should all students study biology? That it is intrinsically important – true as that might be – is not a sufficiently compelling answer. There are a great deal of things that are intrinsically interesting and important that we do not require of all students. That knowledge of biology is important in a society faced with significant policy decisions concerning the environment, for example, or stem cell research is compelling. Knowledge of biology or chemistry or an understanding of technology and its social implications is critical for informed citizenship. It is important for democratic participation in policy decisions that are consequential to us as members of society. If we believe that informed citizenship is the reason that knowledge of the sciences is important for all students, that is, if scientific literacy is critical for the deliberative processes of a democratic society, then this is the objective that should guide the science we require of all students. The familiar introductions to biology, physics, or chemistry serve the purposes of introducing students to the major in these sciences rather well, but I suspect they serve the purposes of scientific understanding for informed citizenship rather badly. The democratic purposes of scientific understanding must influence how the sciences are taught as part of the general education of all students.

Another less obvious but equally important democratic purpose of the education we expect for all students has to do with communication. Everyone believes that a fundamental goal of the education of all students is effective communication. Some of the most impressive recent work on curriculum and on pedagogy has been in written communication and the teaching of writing. The emergence of composition studies programs and new strategies for teaching writing – portfolio approaches, writing labs, writing-to-learn, writing-across-the-curriculum – are familiar features of almost every approach to the teaching of writing in the undergraduate curriculum. I fear, however, that with all of this very valuable attention to writing in the curriculum, we still treat writing and communication generally, as a monological activity, as modes of individual self-expression. More than individual modes of expression, however, communication is fundamentally dialogical. We do not provide sufficient opportunities for our students to become skilled in dialogue.

What might pedagogy that fostered the deliberative aspects of communication look like? It would turn out to be more than teaching the liberating benefits of the liberal arts and merely facilitating the autonomy of students. It would involve more than representing diversity or engaging students in discussion and debate about pressing social issues. As I have suggested throughout this book, one of the compelling aspects of the deliberative turn in democratic theorizing is its focus on the role deliberation plays in consensus formation, given that there are fundamental differences in points of view among deliberators. It is more than merely representing all views, or giving pros and cons, or winning the argument against all comers. Deliberative communication is the process of seeking consensus about collective interests from within the context of disagreement – this is what Gutmann and Thompson have called the "moral economy" of deliberation. I have been experimenting with such a pedagogy in my ethics courses where I structure classes in terms of formulating public policy about such issues as cloning human embryos or genetically modified organisms – issues where there is persistent moral disagreement – and I periodically have students step back and reflect on the process in terms of their understanding of democracy.

The deliberative turn is related in an important way to the issue of diversity. There is general recognition of the importance in a pluralistic democracy of reflecting the diversity of our society and our global context in the curriculum, though campuses sometimes have not been good models of the democratic pluralism we seek to reflect. The culture wars on some campuses are sad testimony to Elshtain's pessimism about our capacity to achieve a new social covenant through which we can reach both consensus and disagreement. One can almost forgive the press for picking up complex issues such as multiculturalism with simpleminded handles such as "political correctness." But we should not be quite so forgiving of the ideological posturing – from both the intellectual right and the left – that has been characteristic of too much of the debate about multiculturalism in the curriculum.

The issue of multiculturalism is difficult. It is difficult because two different but legitimate conceptions of equality that structure the debate seem to contradict one another. One asserts a difference-blind conception of equality in the face of our history of racial, gender, and ethic discrimination. The other asserts the political significance of difference as a requirement for equal recognition. Race matters politically. Gender matters. Sexual identity matters. They cannot be translated without loss into a difference-blind equality. Charles Taylor puts this conflict between different conceptions of what equal recognition requires this way:

[T]he principle of equal respect requires that we treat people in a difference-blind fashion. The fundamental intuition that humans command this respect focuses on what is the same in all. For the other, we have to recognize and even foster particularity. The reproach the first makes to the second is just that it violates the principle of nondiscrimination. The reproach the second makes to the first is that it negates identity by forcing people into a homogeneous mold that is untrue to them. This would be bad enough if the mold were neutral – nobody's mold in particular. But the complaint generally goes further. The claim is that the supposedly neutral set of difference blind principles of the politics of equal dignity is in fact a reflection of one hegemonic culture. As it turns out, then, only the minority or suppressed cultures are being forced to take alien form.[19]

The conflict about multiculturalism in the curriculum is so difficult because both of these conceptions of equal respect are at home in our democratic culture. But both create problems for democracy. The former seems unresponsive to a genuinely pluralistic democracy, and the latter is sometimes defended in undemocratic ways. Despite the cultural and conceptual difficulties, however, faculties have succeeded in incorporating multicultural perspectives in the curriculum. But I worry that it is not always democratic pluralism that is being fostered.

To explain what I mean, let me distinguish what I will call *monadic pluralism* from *democratic pluralism.* If you know the metaphysics of Leibniz, you know that *monad* is his term for the ontologically basic constituents of reality – metaphysical atoms, so to speak. Leibniz's world is a plurality of monads. In one of his most charming descriptions Leibniz tells us that monads "have their windows closed." That is, they have no external relationships with other monads; they merely coexist through preestablished harmony. They unfold their individual histories oblivious to the similar unfolding of monads around them. That is enough of Leibniz to make my distinction. Monadic pluralism recognizes diversity as a brute and enclosed fact and it is satisfied with fostering conditions in which each of us expresses our difference. It fosters articulating and respecting difference with no particular interaction with diverse others. It is this monadic, purely expressive pluralism that too often is the outcome of diversity in the curriculum. It is simply diversity displayed.

Democratic pluralism, however, is not so much expressive as it is dialogical. Or, perhaps better, it is conversational pluralism. I adopt the term *conversation* from the writings of Michael Oakeshott. In his essay, "The Voice of Poetry in the Conversation of Mankind," Oakeshott writes that "education, properly speaking, is an initiation into the skill and partnership of . . . conversation, to recognize the voices, to distinguish the proper occasions of utterance, and in which we acquire the

---

[19] Charles Taylor, "The Politics of Recognition," in *Multiculturalism*, Amy Gutmann, ed. (Princeton: Princeton University Press, 1994), p. 43.

intellectual and moral habits appropriate to conversation."[20] Conversation is a term of art for Oakeshott. Its contrast concept is inquiry. The goal of inquiry is the convergence of discourse – commensurability. Conversation is a partnership where the goal is less a matter of agreement than mutuality of understanding. Iris Marion Young has made similar claims from the point of view of feminism.[21] She objects both to the argumentative construal of deliberation of liberal democrats and to communitarian-oriented deliberative democrats who emphasize a context of shared values as a condition for the possibility of deliberation. The one privileges only one style of discourse. The other overestimates shared values in a pluralistic culture. Both Oakeshott's and Young's views are compatible, I think with Elshtain's interpretation of what a new social covenant must look like: to seek what is common even as we disagree.

Reaching disagreement or differing without disagreeing are two ways of expressing the same communicative skill. And it is a skill that is in exceedingly short supply. What we increasingly lack as a society is the capacity for a conversation of diverse voices. This is what I believe Elshtain means by a new social covenant. It is what Amy Gutmann describes as the very nature of democratic education. According to Gutmann "[T]he most distinctive feature of a democratic theory of education is that it makes a democratic virtue out of our inevitable disagreement over educational problems" (DE, 11). That is, democratic education is not about getting to the truth. It is about the processes that cultivate the democratic dispositions of citizens and the institutions that foster those dispositions in the face of persistent differences. As Alan Keenan has put it, it requires "affirming rather than denying democracy's constitutive incompletion[;] such a mode of democracy would require attitudes of forbearance, self-limitation, and openness to collective self-questioning."[22] A democratic disposition, it seems to me, contains at least the following four elements. First – and less obvious

---

[20] Michael Oakeshott, "The Voice of Poetry in the Conversation of Mankind," in *Rationalism in Politics* (New York: Basic Books, 1962), p. 199.

[21] Iris Marion Young, "Communication and the Other: Beyond Deliberative Democracy," in Seyla Benhabib, *Democracy and Difference: Contesting the Boundaries of the Political* (Princeton: Princeton University Press, 1996), pp. 120–36.

[22] Alan Keenan, *Democracy in Question: Democratic Openness in a Time of Political Closure* (Palo Alto, CA: Stanford University Press, 2003), p. 15.

than it may appear – it must be a disposition *for* democracy, for its aspirations, their incomplete realization, and its constitutively fragile nature. Second, it must include the capacity for democratic communication. Mutuality and respect are the conditions for the possibility of democratic communication, and that is much more than expressing and respecting diversity. It is willingness to seek common ground, given the persistence of differences. Third, it must include the capacity to hold strong convictions while recognizing one's own fallibility and, thus, the fallibility of one's convictions. The ideologues have framed too many of our important debates as if our only alternatives were to embrace the true values or else fall victim to a pernicious relativism: one either has moral conviction or is morally indifferent. It seems to me that the democratic disposition must find its place between the zealots and the nihilists because indifference is as much the enemy of democracy as intolerance. Finally, a democratic disposition is skeptical – not its cynical version, the version fostered by world-weary editorialists and investigative reporters, nor an indifferent skepticism that equally doubts every opinion. I mean the kind of skepticism exemplified by Socrates who could conceive of himself both as son of Athens and gadfly, its true citizen and sharpest critic, stinging Athens to realize its noblest aspirations. It is the skepticism of Montaigne who was capable of appreciating the wide variability of custom and the conventionality of his own beliefs yet embrace them – an embrace that was both committed and critical.

While the culture wars on some campuses merely exemplify the perilous condition of democracy – the difficulty, as Elshtain observes, of reaching disagreement – they do remind us that the curriculum matters and that it is worth disagreeing about. It matters to us, our students, and parents and politicians who support what we do. Debate over the curriculum, what we believe is important for all students to know, can become an object lesson in democratic education if we will let it be. This seems to me the rather sensible recommendation of Gerald Graff's book, *Beyond the Culture Wars*.[23] If we do not construct, through the curriculum and in the classroom, opportunities for students to develop a democratic disposition, if we do not model that

[23] Gerald Graff, *Beyond the Culture Wars: How Teaching the Conflicts Can Revitalize American Education* (New York: W. W. Norton, 1992).

disposition ourselves as we periodically rethink, disagree, and renew our commitments to the purposes of education and the roles of universities and colleges, we will have failed to join the intellectual values of the academy with its democratic possibilities. No matter how successful we are at defending higher education in state houses and donors' living rooms or in designing curriculum, reallocating resources, reforming pedagogy, and assessing outcomes, if we cannot prepare students who can participate meaningfully in democratic deliberation about important issues, and if we cannot do so in ways that preserve the democratic institutions that make our activity possible, we will have failed. Put positively, we do not merely have the opportunity, through rethinking the role of universities and colleges and the democratic purposes of education, to renew our commitment to the importance of education for democracy, but we also have the opportunity to reinvigorate the democratic possibilities of universities and colleges.

Bibliography

Ackerman, Bruce and David Fontana. 2004. "How Jefferson Counted Himself In," *Atlantic Monthly* March: 84–95.

Arendt, Hannah. 1973. *The Origins of Totalitarianism*. New York: Harcourt, Brace and Jovanovich.

———. 1958. *The Human Condition*. Chicago: University of Chicago Press.

Aristotle. 1966. *The Basic Works of Aristotle*. Richard McKeon, trans. New York: Random House.

Baczko, Bronislaw. 1978. "Rousseau and Social Marginality," *Daedalus* 107: 27–40.

Barber, Benjamin. 1994. "Theory and Practice: Democracy and the Philosophers, *History Today* 44: 44–9.

———. 1984. *Strong Democracy: Participatory Politics for a New Age*. Berkeley: University of California Press.

Barkun, Michael. 2002. "Violence in the Name of Democracy: Justification for Separatism on the Radical Right," *Terrorism and Political Violence* 14: 193–208.

Bellah, Robert N. and Richard Madsen, William M. Sullivan, Ann Swindler, and Steven M. Tipton. 1991. *The Good Society*. New York: Alfred A. Knopf.

———. 1985. *Habits of the Heart: Individualism and Commitment in American Life*. Berkeley: University of California Press.

Benhabib, Seyla. 1996. *Democracy and Difference: Contesting the Boundaries of the Political*. Princeton: Princeton University Press.

Benn, S. I. and G. F. Gaus. 1983. *Public and Private in Social Life*. London: St. Martin's Press.

Bennett, William. 1998. *The Death of Outrage: Bill Clinton and the Assault on American Ideals*. New York: The Free Press.

———. 1992. *The De-Valuing of America: The Fight for Our Culture and Our Children*. New York: Simon and Schuster.

Berlin, Isaiah. 1996. *Four Essays on Liberty*. Oxford: Oxford University Press.

Bernstein, Richard. 1992. *The New Constellation.* Cambridge, MA: MIT Press.

Bewes, Timothy. 1997. *Cynicism and Postmodernity.* London: Verso.

Bloom, Allan. 1987. *The Closing of the American Mind: How Higher Education Has Failed Democracy and Impoverished the Souls of Today's Students.* New York: Simon and Schuster.

Bloom, Harold, ed. 1987. *Michel de Montaigne: Modern Critical Views.* New York: Chelsea House Publishers.

Boorstin, Daniel J. 1987. *Hidden History: Exploring our Secret Past.* New York: Vintage Books.

Borre, Ole. 2000. "Critical Issues and Political Alienation in Demark," *Scandinavian Political Studies* 23: 385–410.

Brickhouse, Thomas C. and Nicholas D. Smith. 1989. *Socrates on Trial.* Princeton: Princeton University Press.

Broder, David. 2000. "Historical Election Shaping Up," *The Buffalo News* January 2: 3.

Bufacchi, Vitorrio. 2002. "Sceptical Democracy," *Political Theory* 21: 23–30.

Cappella, Joseph N. and Kathleen Hall Jameson. 1997. *Spiral of Cynicism: The Press and the Public Good.* Oxford: Oxford University Press.

Castoriadis, Cornelius. 1991. *Philosophy, Politics, Autonomy: Essays in Political Philosophy.* Oxford: Oxford University Press.

Charvet, John. 1980. "Rousseau and the Ideal of Community," *History of Political Thought* 1: 69–80.

Conant, James B. 1962. *Thomas Jefferson and the Development of American Public Education.* Berkeley: University of California Press.

Connolly, William E. 1985. "Taylor, Foucault, and Otherness," *Political Theory* 13: 365–76.

——— 1974. *The Terms of Political Discourse.* Princeton: Princeton University Press.

Cooper, John F. 2003. "Taiwan: Democracy Gone Awry?" *Journal of Contemporary China* 12: 145–63.

Cranston, Maurice, ed. 1972. *Hobbes and Rousseau: A Collection of Critical Essays.* New York: Anchor Books.

Dewey, John. 1981. *The Later Works.* Carbondale: Southern Illinois Press.

Diogenes Laertius. 1950. *Lives of Eminent Philosophers.* R. D. Hicks, trans. Cambridge, MA: Harvard University Press.

Dow, Geoff. 2002. "Beyond Cynicism and Desperation," *Australian Journal of International Affairs* 56: 39–46.

Dumont, Louis. 1986. *Essays on Individualism: Modern Ideology in Anthropological Perspective.* Chicago: University of Chicago Press.

Ehrlich, Thomas, ed. 2002. *Civic Responsibility and Higher Education.* Phoenix, AZ: Oryx Press.

Ellis, Joseph J. 1977. *American Sphinx: The Character of Thomas Jefferson.* New York: Alfred A. Knopf.

Elshtain, Jean Bethke. 1995. *Democracy on Trial.* New York: Basic Books.

———. 1981. *Public Man, Private Woman: Women in Social and Political Thought.* Princeton: Princeton University Press.

Euben, Peter J. 1990. *The Tragedy of Political Theory: The Road Not Taken*. Princeton: Princeton University Press.

Fallows, James. 1997. *Breaking the News: How the Media Undermine American Democracy*. New York: Random House.

Flintoff, Everard. 1980. "Pyrrho in India," *Phronesis* 25: 88–108.

Foucault, Michel. 1980a. *Power/Knowledge: Selected Interviews and Other Writings*. Colin Gordon, ed. New York: Pantheon Books.

———. 1980b. *The History of Sexuality, Vol. I*. New York: Random House.

———. 1979. *Discipline and Punish*. New York: Random House.

———. 1965. *Madness and Civilization*. New York: Random House.

Fralin, Richard. 1978. *Rousseau and Representation*. New York: Columbia University Press.

Freedom House. "Democracy's Century: A Survey of Global Political Change in the Twentieth Century," http://www.freedomhouse.org/reports/century.html.

Fukuyama, Francis. 1992. *The End of History and the Last Man*. New York: The Free Press.

Gallie, W. B. 1955–6. "Essentially Contested Concepts," *Proceedings of the Aristotelian Society* 56: 167–98.

Gamarnikov, Eva, ed. 1983. *The Public and the Private*. London: Heinemann.

Goldfarb, Jeffrey C. 1991. *The Cynical Society: The Culture of Politics and the Politics of Culture in American Life*. Chicago: University of Chicago Press.

Graff, Gerald. 1992. *Beyond the Culture Wars: How Teaching the Conflicts Can Re-vitalize American Education*. New York: Norton Publishing.

Gutmann, Amy and Denis Thomas. 1996. *Democracy and Disagreement*. Cambridge, MA: Harvard University Press.

———, ed. 1994. *Multiculturalism*. Princeton: Princeton University Press.

———. 1987. *Democratic Education*. Princeton: Princeton University Press.

———. 1980. *Liberal Equality*. Cambridge: Cambridge University Press.

Habermas, Jurgen. 1989. *Structural Transformation of the Public Sphere: An Inquiry into a Category of Bourgeois Society*. Cambridge, MA: MIT Press.

———. 1987. *Philosophical Discourse of Modernity*. Cambridge, MA: MIT Press.

———. 1979. *Communication and the Evolution of Society*. Boston: Beacon Press.

Hamilton, Alexander, James Madison, and John Jay. 1983. *The Federalist Papers*. New York: Bantam Books.

Hart, Vivien. 1978. *Distrust and Democracy: Political Distrust in Britain and America*. Cambridge: Cambridge University Press.

Heidegger, Martin. 1977. *The Question Concerning Technology and Other Essays*. New York: Garland.

Held, David. 1987. *Models of Democracy*. Palo Alto, CA: Stanford University Press.

Hiley, David R. 1988. *Philosophy in Question: Essays on a Pyrrhonian Theme*. Chicago: University of Chicago Press.

Hiley, David R., James F. Bohman, and Richard Schusterman. 1991. *The Interpretive Turn: Philosophy, Science, Culture*. Ithaca, NY: Cornell University Press.

Jaeger, Werner. 1943. *Paideia: Ideals of Greek Culture Vol. II*. Oxford: Oxford University Press.

John S. Dryzek. 2002. *Deliberative Democracy and Beyond: Liberals, Critics, Contestations.* Oxford: Oxford University Press.

Jones, A. H. M. 1986. *Athenian Democracy.* Baltimore: The Johns Hopkins University.

Kateb, George. 1992. *The Inner Ocean: Individualism and Democratic Culture.* Ithaca, NY: Cornell University Press.

Kaufman, Jason. 2002. *For the Common Good? American Civic Life and the Golden Age of Fraternity.* Oxford: Oxford University Press.

Keenan, Alan. 2003. *Democracy in Question: Democratic Openness in a Time of Political Closure.* Palo Alto, CA: Stanford University Press.

Kegan, Donald. 1991. *Pericles of Athens and the Birth of Democracy.* New York: The Free Press.

Ketchman, Ralph. 1987. *Individualism and Public Life: A Modern Dilemma.* Oxford: Oxford University Press.

Kramer, Roderick M. 1998. "Paranoid Cognition in Social Systems: Thinking and Acting in the Shadow of Doubt," *Personality and Social Psychology Review* 2: 251–75.

Kraut, Richard. 1984. *Socrates and the State.* Princeton: Princeton University Press.

Kuhn, Thomas. 1977. *The Essential Tension: Selected Studies in Scientific Tradition and Change.* Chicago: University of Chicago Press.

Kundera, Milan. 1984. *The Unbearable Lightness of Being.* New York: Harper and Row.

Lane, Melissa. 2002. "Was Socrates a Democrat?" *History Today* 42–7.

Lasch, Christopher. 1984. *The Minimal Self: Psychic Survival in Troubled Times.* New York: W. W. Norton.

———. 1979. *The Culture of Narcissism: American Life in the Age of Diminishing Expectations.* New York: W. W. Norton.

Laurensen, J. C. 1989. "Scepticism and Intellectual Freedom: The Philosophical Foundations of Kant's Politics of Publicity," *History of Political Theory* 10: 439–45.

Levine, David Michel, ed. 1987. *Pathologies of the Modern Self: Postmodern Studies on Narcissism, Schizophrenia, and Depression.* New York: New York University Press.

MacIntyre, Alasdair. 1981. *After Virtue.* Notre Dame: University of Notre Dame Press.

Malachowiski, Alan R. 1990. *Reading Rorty.* Oxford: Basil Blackwell.

Manet, Pierre. 1994. *An Intellectual History of Liberalism.* Princeton: Princeton University Press.

Mendus, Susan, ed. 1988. *Justifying Toleration.* Cambridge: Cambridge University Press.

Merleau-Ponty, Maurice. 1964. "Reading Montaigne." In *Signs*, Richard C. McClary, trans., 198–210. Evanston, IL: Northwestern University Press.

Mill, John Stuart. 1978. *On Liberty.* Indianapolis: Hackett Publishing.

Mohr, Richard D. 1992. *Gay Ideas: Outing and Other Controversies.* Boston: Beacon Press.

Montaigne, Michel de. 1965. *The Complete Works of Montaigne*. Donald M. Frame, trans. Palo Alto, CA: Stanford University Press.

Munn, Mark. 2000. *The School of Athens: Athens in the Age of Socrates*. Berkeley: University of California Press.

Norris, Pippa, ed. 1999. *Critical Citizens: Global Support for Democratic Governance*. Oxford: Oxford University Press.

Oakeshott, Michael. 1996. *The Politics of Faith and the Politics of Scepticism*. Timothy Fuller, ed. New Haven: Yale University Press.

———. 1962. *Rationalism in Politics*. New York: Basic Books.

Pitkin, Hanna Feniche. 1981. "Justice: On Relating Private and Public," *Political Theory* 9: 327–52.

Plato. 1971. *The Collected Dialogues of Plato*. Princeton: Princeton University Press.

Postmodernity Project. The State of Disunion: 1996 Survey of American Political Culture, http://minerva.acc.Virginia.EDU/-postmod/survey Home.html.

Putman, Robert D. 2000. *Bowling Alone: The Collapse and Revival of American Community*. New York: Simon and Schuster.

Rajchman, John. 1985. *Michel Foucault: The Freedom of Philosophy*. New York: Columbia University Press.

Rawls, John. 1993. *Political Liberalism*. New York: Columbia University Press.

Readings, Bill. 1997. *The University in Ruins*. Cambridge, MA: Harvard University Press.

Riley, Patrick. 1982. *Will and Political Legitimacy*. Cambridge, MA: Harvard University Press.

Rorty, Richard. 1998. *Achieving Our Country*, Cambridge, MA: Harvard University Press.

———. 1989. *Contingency, Irony and Solidarity*. Cambridge: Cambridge University Press.

Rosanvallon, Pierre. 1995. "The History of the Word 'Democracy' in France," *The Journal of Democracy* 4: 140–54.

Rousseau, Jean-Jacques. 1979. *Emile, or On Education*. Allan Bloom, trans. New York: Basic Books.

———. 1978a. Benjamin R. Barber and Janis Forman, trans. "A Preface to 'Narcisse: Or the Lover of Himself,'" *Political Theory* 6: 537–42.

———. 1978b. *On the Social Contract*. Roger D. Masters, ed. and Judith R. Masters, trans. New York: St. Martin's Press.

———. 1968. *Politics and the Arts: Letter to M. d'Alembert on the Theatre*. Allan Bloom, trans. New York: Cornell University Press.

———. 1964. *The First and Second Discourses*. Roger D. and Judith R. Masters, trans. New York: St. Martin's Press.

———. 1954. *The Confessions*. J. M. Cohen, trans. Baltimore: Penguin Books, Inc.

Sandel, Michael J. 1996. *Democracy's Discontent: America in Search of a Public Philosophy*. Cambridge, MA: Harvard University Press.

———. 1984. *Liberalism and Its Critics*. New York: New York University Press.

————. 1982. *Liberalism and the Limits of Justice.* Cambridge: Cambridge University Press.

Saxonhouse, Arlene. 1992. *Fear of Diversity: The Birth of Political Science in Greek Thought.* Chicago: University of Chicago Press.

Schaefer, David Lewis. 1990. *The Political Philosophy of Montaigne.* Ithaca, NY: Cornell University Press.

Sen, Amartya. 1999. "Democracy as a Universal Value," *Journal of Democracy* 10: 3–17.

Sennett, Richard. 1978. *The Fall of Public Man: On the Social Psychology of Capitalism.* New York: Vantage Books.

Sextus Empiricus. 1933. *Outlines of Pyrrhonism.* R. G. Bury, trans. Cambridge. MA: Harvard University Press.

Shaklar, Judith N. 1991. *American Citizenship: The Quest for Inclusion.* Cambridge, MA: Harvard University Press.

Skocpol, Theda and Morris P. Fiorina, eds. 1999. *Civic Engagement in American Democracy.* Washington, DC: Brookings Institution Press.

Slaughter, Sheila and Larry L. Leslie, eds. 1997. *Academic Capitalism: Politics, Policies, and the Entrepreneurial University.* Baltimore: The Johns Hopkins Press.

Sloterdijk, Peter. 1988. *Critique of Cynical Reason.* London: Verso.

Starobinski, Jean. 1985. *Montaigne in Motion.* Chicago: University of Chicago Press.

Stone, I. F. 1988. *The Trial of Socrates.* Boston: Little Brown and Co.

Sunstein, Cass R. 2003. *Why Societies Need Dissent.* Cambridge, MA: Harvard University Press.

Talmon, J. L. 1960. *The Origins of Totalitarian Democracy.* New York: Praeger Books.

Taylor, Charles. 1998. "The Dynamics of Democratic Exclusion," *Journal of Democracy* 9: 143–57.

————. 1995. *Philosophical Arguments.* Cambridge, MA: Harvard University Press.

————. 1992. *The Ethics of Authenticity.* Cambridge, MA: Harvard University Press.

————. 1987. *Philosophical Papers.* Vol. 2. Cambridge: Cambridge University Press.

Thucydides. 1972. *History of the Peloponnesian Wars.* Rex Warner, trans. New York: Penguin Books.

Tilley, Arthur Augustus. 1922. "Montaigne's Interpreters." In *Studies in French Renaissance,* p. 17. Cambridge: Cambridge University Press.

Tocqueville, Alexis de. 1990. *Democracy in America.* 2 vols. New York: Vintage Books.

Utne, Leif. 2003. "Don't Cry for Argentina," *Utne Reader* January–February: 17–19.

Vander Waerdt, Paul A. ed. 1994. *The Socratic Movement.* Ithaca, NY: Cornell University Press.

Villa, Dana. 2001. *Socratic Citizenship.* Princeton: Princeton University Press.

Vlastos, Gregory. 1991. *Socrates: Ironist and Moral Philosopher.* Ithaca, NY: Cornell University Press.

————. 1983. "The Historical Socrates and Athenian Democracy," *Political Theory* 11: 495–518.

Wagner, Judy. 1986. *The Search for Signs of Intelligent Life in the Universe.* New York: Harper and Row.

Walzer, Michael. 1983. *Spheres of Justice.* London: Blackwell.

West, Cornel. 2004. *Democracy Matters.* New York: Penguin Books.

————. 1993. *Race Matters.* Boston: Beacon Press.

Whitman, Walt. 1950. "Democratic Vistas." In *Leaves of Grass and Selected Prose.* John Kouwenhoven, ed. New York: Modern Library.

Wills, Gary. 1999. *A Necessary Evil: A History of American Distrust of Government.* New York: Simon and Schuster.

Wolfe, Alan. 1977. *The Limits of Legitimacy: Political Contradictions in Contemporary Capitalism.* New York: The Free Press.

Wood, Gordon S. 1993. *The Radicalism of the American Revolution.* New York: Vintage Books.

Index